What Every Stude

COLLEGE
UNDER
COVER

MERRICK JON MARINO

WHARTON PUBLISHING

Del Mar, CA   *1993*

Publisher's Cataloging-in-Publication Data

Marino, Merrick J.
    College undercover: what every student needs to know/Merrick Jon Marino.
    p. cm.
    ISBN 1-56912-098-6
        1. Study, Method of — Handbooks, manuals, etc. 2. College students — United States — Life skills guides. 3. Universities and colleges — United States. I. Title.

LB2395.M37 1993   378´ .170281
                QB193-20424

Editor .... *Rebecca Jaurigue*
Layout Design ..... *Michele Jansen*

Printed in the United States of America.

Acknowledgment

It's been a long haul that I never could have endured without the support and encouragement I received along the way. Collaboration has proved to be an essential element of this book. Many thanks to all those who offered their input. From a pool of ideas, a book is spawned.

Special thanks to Jim (Dad) Marino, Julie (Mom) Buchanan, the rest of my family, Bonnie Kristell, Frontline Video & Film, Tom Baldauf, Holly Denton, Rob McAdam, Samantha Wright, Robert Agee, and all those who assisted or took part in interviews.

And a very special thanks to Rebecca Jaurigue, who added such an incredible amount to this project. Her dedication is apparent throughout every page that follows.

TABLE OF CONTENTS

Introduction ix

I. Your Job as College Student 1

    A. Recommendations for Success 2

        1. Attendance 4

        2. Writing Skills 5

        3. Reading 9

        4. Note-Taking 11

        5. Time-Management 11

        6. Flexibility 17

        7. Balance 18

B. School Policies 19

    1. Drop/Add 19

    2. Pass/No Pass 23

    3. Transfer Credit 25

    4. Waivers 27

    5. Incompletes 28

    6. Disputing Grades 29

II. Beginning 33

A. New Student Orientations/Registration 33

B. Orientation 36

C. Financial Aid 38

D. Classes 40

    1. Days 42

    2. Units 45

    3. Numbering System 46

    4. Class Structures 47

        A. Lecture Courses 47

        B. Small Classes 49

        C. Small Lectures 49

    5. Coursework 50

E. Major 54

III. Getting Started 57

    1. Here You Ço 57

    2. There I Went 58

    3. Arriving 58

IV. First Year Classes 63

    A. Fall Semester 64

    B. Spring Semester 73

V. Tips from Experience 77

    1. Take Your Assignments Seriously 77

    2. Extra Credit Opportunities 78

    3. Maybe I Don't Have To Do Everything? 78

    4. Notice Patterns 80

    5. Know Your Strengths and Weaknesses 82

VI. First Year Life 85

    A. Observations 91

    B. The Greek System 101

VII. Attitude and Atmosphere 107

Conclusion 113

INTRODUCTION

I am writing this book the summer after graduating from the University of Southern California (USC) with a Bachelor of Arts degree in Broadcast Journalism and Minor in Cinema-Television. Out of high school, I was an average student. I turned my performance around in college as I developed my own system of studying geared for the typical university class. As a result, I graduated Phi Beta Kappa (national honor society) and Magna Cum Laude with a cumulative G.P.A. of 3.76. I am definitely not the type of person who "loves" school or learning all the time. My experiences at USC proved to me that you don't have to be a genius or a completely dedicated student to succeed in college. You can, and should, have a life outside of your schoolwork to complement your studies.

This book prepares you for college by providing several recommendations and shortcuts to help you make the transition. Everything is based on my personal experiences after just completing the whole process:

- Descriptions of typical classes
- Study techniques to maximize your time and minimize stress
- Hints on using school policies to your advantage
- Overview of my first year — including excerpts from some of my first year coursework
- Tips on what to expect during the first year of college
- Suggestions on how a student's attitude and atmosphere play a positive role in the college experience

I remember when I was first accepted to USC. The summer before attending, I had no idea what to expect. Talking to people helped a little, but on the first day of classes, when I walked into a lecture hall with five hundred other students, I realized I was lost.

For better or for worse, you have to get used to the structure and requirements of university classes right away. I know that when I left high school and started college, I would have loved something or someone to explain exactly what I could expect.

However, most students are too busy finding a job or getting ready for graduate school to document their experiences, let alone spend the time explaining how they excelled — if that's the case. So I am writing promptly the summer after graduating, while everything is fresh in my memory. Now I can look back at my first year and know what would have helped me prepare for college classes and life.

Every college or university around the nation has differing policies and classes. However, the general education requirements and class structure are roughly the same throughout. The principles I suggest can be applied to whatever situation you may encounter from the first year on. This flexibility might be necessary, for example, once you select and begin courses in a specific major and find that these courses are geared toward that particular specialization. Usually, most of your major courses will be taken during the third and fourth years (or fifth and sixth too, if necessary).

After the first year of study, though, most people have already developed their own approach to coursework. *So the first year is crucial, because if you develop successful techniques, you may apply them throughout your college career in general education and major courses.* However, if you have poor study techniques, you will struggle through your final years trying to correct mistakes and find a comfortable routine.

Each college and university has innumerable differences between them: private schools are often unlike public schools, big schools unlike small schools, and schools away from home unlike schools in your town. The best source of information regarding requirements and policies for your particular school is usually that school's official catalogue (Look for one at your school's admissions office, student center, or campus bookstore).

Keep in mind that there are thousands of colleges and universities in the United States alone. The information in this catalogue cannot apply to every one exactly. However, it will give you an idea of what to expect during your first year, and will also provide helpful suggestions that can be applied to basic general education and many major courses at any school.

I believe that my techniques will work for you. I am not a professor researching study techniques, or a school official giving popular advice on succeeding in a college or university. I am a student who just did it. So take this material as if you were talking in-depth to a student who just graduated and did really well. That's me, and I'll explain many of the finer points about college that you will soon experience.

Much of what I suggest is common sense. However, I feel many students overlook the obvious. There is no need to drive yourself crazy or stress out in school. If you manage your time and provide yourself with a positive atmosphere for studying, there should be few problems.

Remember that school is sometimes unfair. You may not learn some subjects as quickly or easily as others. Or, your background in some subjects may not match up to others. However, there are ways to avoid such difficulties before you get in too far over your head. (The ins-and-outs of the fine art of class selection are discussed in the drop/add section of the book.)

If you just want to get through college with a minimum of stress or effort, you can. If you want to succeed with a minimum of stress, you can. If you want to work to become an expert in your selected field, you can do that, too. The choice is yours. This book will especially help those who want to do well in school, while maintaining precious free time to enjoy some of life's non-academic pleasures and activities.

I YOUR JOB AS COLLEGE STUDENT

In order to take college seriously, you should consider this position your job for the next four years or more. Even if you work through college, your title is still "college student." By making the most of your student career, you increase the likelihood of favorable options when you graduate.

If regarding college as a career motivates you, consider these direct comparisons.

- Orientation is your training session.
- Attendance is showing up to work.
- Schoolwork is getting the work done.
- Your schoolmates are co-workers. You must work with them, competing for top positions.
- Your instructors are supervisors. You must demonstrate your abilities and dedication to them.
- Finally, you must decide what you want out of the career and do your best to meet your goals.

Like any job, the transition is difficult. You want to succeed from the very start. In almost any endeavor, the way you approach the beginning can determine the outcome. Unlike a career, though, you won't be fired from college if you fail (in college, academic probation is usually the result of poor performance). Your results may play a major role in future career or academic pursuits.

Many techniques for succeeding in college are the same as the factors for success in careers or work situations.

- Demonstrate reliability and show up every day (attendance).
- Communicate effectively and persuasively (writing skills).
- Stay updated on current and future trends (reading).
- Manage your individual responsibilities, commitments, and expectations (note-taking).
- Perform work duties efficiently (time management).
- Handle new problems or opportunities as they arise (flexibility).
- Continue enjoying your favorite hobbies and activities, and limit stress (balance).

College is your life for four or more years, so consider it your job. And like any job, you want to do your best.

A. Recommendations for Success

As you begin your college career, you may find that class structures and requirements are new and difficult. The key to success in college is establishing your own method for studying that works for you. So the first year is extremely important to develop effective study techniques and adjust to the new style of coursework.

In my observations, most people who succeeded in their first years of college continued this success throughout their college careers. And students who performed poorly in their first year often maintained that pattern throughout college. It is possible to overcome beginning mistakes, but life and school will be much easier, if you establish a productive approach to handling college life and studies right away.

> "The number one thing I noticed top students all have is self-motivation. If there is any variable at all in all levels of school among top students, it is self-motivation.
>
> The secondary trait is study skills — the ability to retrieve information from class and the reading and put it in their own words. Also, taking good notes and looking at them after class, and understanding and finding information in the book."
>
> — *Scott Swearingen*
> *Assistant Instructor , Introductory Sociology*
> *University of Texas at Austin*

The study techniques I developed in my four years of college allowed me to live a comfortable lifestyle, while earning top grades in almost every class. In fact, I studied as little as possible without jeopardizing my course grades. However, even studying that much required a great deal of hard work and discipline. Do not let this process discourage you. If you're fascinated by certain subjects and want to learn more, do it.

Instead of dismissing my suggestions, come up with a viable substitute. Usually, if you discount an approach because it requires too much time or work, this neglect will show in your course grades.

Remember, this system worked for me. If you can work the following recommendations into your own system, I am confident you will earn respectable grades and honors.

1. Attendance

The strongest recommendation I can possibly give is to attend every class, including lab/discussions. *An extraordinary amount of learning and preparation is accomplished just by sitting in the classroom, listening to the professor speak, and actively taking notes.*

When you go back to study your notes, you recall the information faster after already hearing it once. Copying someone else's notes or making copies of notes is not as effective as hearing and writing the notes yourself. Also, on tests or papers, the professor may ask for information that you do not have in your notes, but you recall hearing the material in class. An absent student has no chance to answer such a question, or include this information in a paper. So you have an immediate advantage over students who miss classes. They might either buy lecture notes, or make copies of notes from classmates. You may be able to get away with missing a few classes, but if this practice is common, it will show.

At many schools, you can purchase lecture notes for certain classes. Sometimes, professors make class notes available. However, prepared class notes are most often sold by independent groups that solicit their products through fliers and cards on campus.

Buying class notes may be useful for some people, but this approach is not always an effective, or reliable, method for learning and understanding course material.

My theory is, "What's it gonna hurt by just showing up, and taking notes in each class?" Besides, this is simple. There is plenty of time during the day to have fun, take a nap, or just relax. Although, during mid-terms and finals, you probably will not have as much free time.

I believe that students who show up to every class, take good notes, turn in their papers or assignments, and study for their exams using just the information from sitting through classes will at least earn a "C," or passing grade, in that course. If you insist on doing nothing else, go to every class and take notes. You should be able to get by. Often, students are pressured to miss classes with invitations to hang out with friends or temptations to sleep in. *Compromises you make in order to attend class will pay off in the long run.*

Remember, attendance is part of your job as a college student. Showing up to class is one of the easiest things you can do. It makes the rest of your job much easier. Think ahead, and you'll agree that attending class is a no-loss situation.

2. Writing Skills

Writing well is the most important skill you can develop to succeed in most classes. No matter what major you choose, you need to write. The fastest way to a turn off a professor or prospective employer is with poor writing skills.

Professors are impressed by effective writing skills. Writing well is not an easy task, though. You will compete with other students who have a range of writing abilities (depending on their natural talent and the level and quality of their prior education). *With the amount of papers and essay tests in most classes, writing is an essential key for success in most classes.*

If you had trouble in the past with writing assignments, do whatever you can to improve this skill.

Here are some options:

- Go to writing centers on campus.
- Work with a writing tutor.
- See instructors during office hours about how to improve.
- Pay careful attention to comments on papers and tests to find consistent problems.
- Practice writing when you can.

> "My top students show a willingness to see me in my office hours, and accept that they have room to change and improve. They must put in effort to improving, and revising their work.
>
> In one of my classes . . . a girl revised all her papers without me asking her to, and then came in to discuss the papers. She went from a D+ to an A."
>
> — *David Morse*
> *Assistant Lecturer, Freshman Composition*
> *University of Southern California*

The earlier you develop good writing skills, the better your results will be in your classes throughout your studies and later in your career.

Some basic reminders:

- Read the writing assignment carefully. Determine exactly what is required. Then address those issues.

- Read your papers aloud to yourself. Ask yourself if they make sense, lead toward the conclusion you want to make, and are constructed with clear sentences and strong vocabulary. See if you can replace five words with one equally effective word, or replace five sentences with one equally effective sentence.

- Have a friend read the paper and get critical feedback from them.

Each professor and teacher's assistant (T.A.) prefers different writing styles, and has their own ideas about how papers should be written. So it's your job to find out as much as possible about these preferences before turning in your paper.

Effective writing techniques are appreciated by every instructor. Good writing is good writing wherever you go. And, if nothing else works, find friends or classmates who have greater success with writing assignments, and have them read and help you with your writing assignments. Of course, this type of assistance is, to be blunt, impossible when taking an essay exam in a closed classroom, which is usually the case for mid-terms and finals. You're on your own for tests. So do everything you can to develop the skills yourself.

In short, good writing helps you with every aspect of coursework, and even allows you to make your way through tests and papers you do not fully understand.

Computers vs. Typewriters

What you write with may actually contribute to your success, along with helping you save precious time.

Since most general education courses require some sort of writing assignments, a computer can be invaluable for saving, revising, and printing papers. My first year in school, I only had a typewriter, and it was a pain in the neck. After handwriting all my papers, I then had to type them up.

With a computer or word processor, you type the paper once and revise it on the screen. Very simple and efficient.

Unfortunately, the computer vs. typewriter vs. nothing decision may be determined solely by economics. Even if you are not in a position to purchase a computer or typewriter, there are other options. Most schools have computer centers open to all students. These computer centers may use Macintosh or IBM compatible computers. Call the admissions office or student center at your school to find out which system is used.

At my school, students using the computer center facilities supplied their own disks and paid for each page of printing.

A major drawback to relying on computer centers is the crowds during the middle of the semester and just before finals, when most papers are due. So if students do not prepare beforehand, they often face long hours of waiting. Sometimes, students are forced to turn in papers late, and suffer whatever penalties the instructor slaps on late assignments.

Another option for students to consider is borrowing a friend's computer. The obvious problem is that this friend may have to work on his or her own paper when you need to work on yours.

Whatever you do, make sure you plan far in advance how to write and print your papers. Remember, almost every instructor at every school requires typewritten or printed papers — nothing handwritten, with no exceptions.

3. Reading

The syllabus, or course outline, lists required books for a course, along with reading assignments. For students, like me, who like to read as little as possible for classes, there are shortcuts. However, for people who love to read everything for classes, there's no way to go wrong. You have a definite advantage over most of your classmates.

Reading Shortcuts

Now for the students who want to read only what's absolutely necessary. First, talk to other students who took the class before. Find out how much reading is required in the course and how much of that reading is necessary in order to do well. The replies will be a combination of "No, you don't have to read anything for papers or tests," "Yeah, you get asked some questions from the reading," or "The tests and papers are totally based on the reading, so read everything — plus there are weekly quizzes."

Remember, although other students are a good source of information, you are trusting their opinion based on past experience. Don't blame anyone if the information is slightly off, because this is part of the risk you take with shortcuts.

The best advice is to just do all the readings for every course. Again, these assignments are another responsibility that goes along with the job description of "college student."

An easy way out is to keep up with the readings until the first paper and exam. Then you can see for yourself how much information the professor or T.A. wants from the readings. If you're not quite sure, keep reading just to be safe.

I noticed that *students who often got good grades outlined each chapter or reading assignment throughout the semester.* This technique is especially effective in classes where all the tests are based on memorizing facts. However, I never made outlines and did fine.

In classes where reading was crucial, I highlighted important statements as I read. Then before test time, I sat down about one week before and rewrote my notes for each class session, including a section on the readings that coordinated with that class session. For example, if I was copying my notes from the Philosophy lecture on October 12, I would also go through the book and add any important highlighted information from the readings required for the October 12 lecture.

This approach may sound time-consuming, but it worked for me. Usually, I spent a weekend or two to three days preparing my study notes. From that point on, I recalled much of the information from having copied it. Studying was a breeze. All I had to do was read through my notes a few times a day until test time. Believe me, other students were always jealous when they saw my study sheets.

Everybody learns in different ways. I rewrote information because I don't remember anything after just one pass. So figure out what triggers your mind before you face a test where you go blank. You will know what works best for you.

4. Note-taking

My theory to note-taking is to *take down everything that sounds important or could possibly show up on a test.* You never know what a professor or T.A. will ask for on a test or in a paper. So if you have notes of everything, you can't miss.

Taking notes is not copying every word the professor says. Rather, copy down anything that sounds relevant to major topics of discussion. *Check the course syllabus to see what major topics the professor or T.A. has highlighted for the semester or quarter.* I always hated looking at a question on a test and realizing I didn't even have that information in my notes.

So write down whatever you think you may need later. For a one-hour lecture, I usually averaged about four pages of notes. Use your own judgement to determine what information is useful for each class. If not quite sure, err on the side of taking more notes. As time goes on, you will get a better feel for what information is necessary for exams and papers.

5. Time-Management

Effective time-management should allow students enough time to complete all the necessary work to do well in class, have free time for leisure activities, and get a healthy amount of sleep. *So you must make the most of the time you have for your studies.* If you decide on intense majors like electrical engineering or molecular biology, the likelihood of free time is less than most other students.

"I suggest that students stick to a consistent schedule. First, you stick to the things that are non-negotiable each day — like classes, club meetings, study groups, and time to eat. Then you fill the space left open.

To manage time well, you shouldn't leave any time open. Put in everything. You should schedule study times — what to study at what time — and even fun time, including leisure and exercise.

> — *Gary Tedeschi*
> *Staff Psychologist*
> *University of San Diego*

Time-management experts can offer great advice, but the ultimate test is whether or not a system works for you. *The best approach is take whatever suggestions you can find, and work them into an individualized system that fits in with your personality, lifestyle, and schedule.*

In my approach, I overbudgeted time way ahead and hoped to finish most of what I set out to do. In other words, *for each assignment or exam, I overestimated how much time it would take to complete the work.*

For example, I told myself that to complete a six-page paper, I needed to start one week before it was due and spend eight hours of writing. However, in reality, I only needed to start three days ahead of time and spend four hours writing.

So, working under the assumption of my overestimated guidelines, I finished the paper about three days before the due date. This way, I usually had time to proofread papers and have friends proofread them. Also, I eliminated the stress involved with working under last minute conditions. Another advantage from this process, if done early enough, is to turn in a paper early to professors or T.A.'s, and get them to hand it back in time to make corrections before the due date. Unfortunately, I could never get myself to work that far in advance. However, I know people who did, and it almost always resulted in high scores or grades on those papers.

If you've ever seen Notre Dame football coach Lou Holtz discuss his opponents, this process is similar. Coach Holtz never underestimates any competitor, no matter how much his team over-matches the opposing side. So if the team excels, he feels great. However, if an unexpected challenge comes up, the team is prepared.

This time-management process also considers every assignment or exam as a worthy opponent. By preparing ahead of time, the student is ready for any unanticipated problems. So the student usually excels on easier assignments and exams, and can handle more difficult material.

Now I might sound like a parent or teacher here, but this advice is relevant. When you sit down to do your work — DO IT. Don't visit people. Don't call people on the phone. Don't watch T.V. DO YOUR WORK. Or at least, keep your distractions down. I admit I can't sit for three hours straight, and just work. You may have to get up and walk around, get a snack, or take a short break, but use your work time effectively. If you do, guess what happens? You get things done.

Since it's your job, it is your responsibility to find the work environment in college that allows you to achieve your desired results.

I would also break up studying for one class with work from other classes and free time. Here's a typical busy day for me, if I had two one-hour classes, a two-hour class, a three-hour paper, and an hour of reading to catch up on.

8:00 a.m.	—	Wake up
8:30 - 9:00 a.m.	—	Eat breakfast
9:00 - 9:50	—	Class
10:00 - 11:00 a.m.	—	Work on paper
11:00 - 11:30 a.m.	—	Read
11:30 - 1:50 p.m.	—	Eat lunch
2:00 - 3:50 p.m.	—	Class
4:00 - 4:50 p.m.	—	Class
5:00 - 6:00 p.m.	—	Workout
6:00 - 6:30 p.m.	—	Work on paper
6:30 - 8:00 p.m.	—	Eat dinner
8:00 - 8:30 p.m.	—	Read
8:30 - 10:00 p.m.	—	Work on paper
10:00 - 11:30 p.m.	—	Go out
12:00 a.m.	—	Go to sleep

I split my time, so I was not stuck working on my paper or reading for long periods. This technique is also geared toward my lifestyle — i.e. time for working out and long periods of time for meals (which is a great way to relax).

Sometimes, you may not have as much flexibility, because of sports teams, social clubs, or part-time jobs.

"We encourage students to utilize time during the day. Many students are not used to studying during the day. However, evening time gets eaten up with social or other commitments."

— *Dr. Hugh Pates*
Psychologist
University of California, San Diego

Figure out what you need to get done, and how much time you have available. To make it work, though, you must be productive during that allotted time. Just do it and get it over with. Planning ahead and budgeting more time than necessary is a great way to get things done early without too much stress. Most likely, you end up with more free time than you thought, which is always a nice treat.

Certain times during the semester, usually around midterms and finals, papers and exams stack up, and you have a great deal to get done. Then you will see everybody start to stress. Worrying about everything you have to do gets you nowhere. Some people work better under stress — that's fine, but not always healthy. Those students who manage their time productively will have prepared for the rush way ahead of time. They just have to put in a little more time than usual for a week or so.

Parents, teachers, and even you, know that waiting until the last-minute rarely ever works. You'll probably find yourself constantly pressed for time, and incapable of doing your best work. You don't have to make life a major pain. Eventually, the work has to be done, so do it sooner rather than later. You can get it off your mind to allow for more enjoyable activities.

Using this technique for managing my time, I completed my four years of college and still had time for most activities that I wanted — working out five days a week, playing lacrosse for two years, playing drums, almost never staying up late to do schoolwork, visiting my family in San Diego often, and working twenty hours a week during my senior year.

If you manage your available time, you can have a great deal of free time. However, if you overcommit yourself to other activities, there probably won't be enough hours in the day to get everything you need done. Unfortunately, schoolwork often suffers under these circumstances.

My system is not the only way to manage your time, but it worked for me. The idea is only to manage your time in a way that works for you. Remember that any system should result in making the absolute most of the limited amount of time you have available.

6. Flexibility

You often have to adapt what you know to various situations on tests or papers.

Every test question you encounter will not come directly from your notes or the book. Neither will every paper topic. So you need to be flexible with your understanding of course material. You may often be asked to expand on what you have learned in class and from the reading.

Sometimes, exam questions and paper topics come straight from lecture material or required readings. In these cases, you still have to put in plenty of hours to decide and memorize which information is important.

In preparing for tests and papers, you must review, know, and understand class material. After you have this necessary information down, you can apply it to any related question that comes up. This process requires a little thinking.

The best and only way to have all the flexibility you need is to be thoroughly prepared. Make study guides from class notes and readings. Go over them as many times as it takes to know everything on them. Or use whatever study approach you find best to learn and understand course material. Also, relax in exam and writing situations, because this is the best way for you to show what and how much you know.

An entire section on attitude and atmosphere appears later in the book, and provides further insight. Keep this in mind until you get there: Do your best, and there's nothing more anyone can ask of you. I believe that, since you have yourself to answer to, it is important to be happy with the amount of time and effort you put in to your college studies. After all, you live with your results. This philosophy helped me get by, and also made any results acceptable.

7. Balance

If you're like me, or like many others, you can't spend all your time studying and worrying about school. So planning your time effectively is essential. You will have available time to get away. If you love studying all the time, skip to the next section.

If you can put school away at times, the time you spend in school and in studying is more beneficial and productive. When people get burned out, they lose focus. So get away when you can. Spend time doing things you enjoy. Of course, don't take necessary time from your school commitments to get away. Take the extra time after you have everything done.

What should you do to get away? Anything and everything you enjoy. I enjoyed going home to San Diego for weekends, seeing movies, going out for dinner, working out, playing racquetball, playing lacrosse, playing softball, or just hanging out and doing nothing. However, I remained disciplined and never engaged in these activities, unless I had everything finished, or I knew I had plenty of time to make up what I missed.

Doing things you enjoy is always hard to pass up, but *if you want to succeed, you sometimes have to sacrifice play for work.* Also, be careful not to put everything off. This time adds up, and gets to a point where you're too far behind to catch up. However, I believe if you spend your time wisely, you will have time for fun.

B. School Policies

As you enter your college or university, you will find a whole new world of regulations and policies.

After becoming familiar with the regulations and policies at my school, I discovered that I could use many of these policies to my advantage. For each policy I discuss, however, you should look into whether or not your school has the same or similar policy.

1. Drop/Add

The drop/add policy at my school allows students to drop or add any classes within the first three weeks of classes without the class appearing on their transcripts.

During the 4th through 12th weeks of class, students can drop classes and receive a "W" (withdrawal) on their transcript and no credit for the course. However, a "W" does not reflect in a student's grade point average.

Withdrawing from a course is often used as a safety measure for students who are fearful of failing or receiving a poor grade in a course. Students can usually repeat the course for a grade.

I often took advantage of the opportunity to drop/add classes. Usually, I changed at least two of my courses every semester for my first two years. When I took my general education (G.E.) classes, I could select from a number of courses to satisfy the same requirement. As far as I was concerned, there was no reason to stay in a class I didn't like.

My reasons for switching classes were numerous:

- The subject did not interest me.
- The teacher was disagreeable.
- I had a difficult semester and wanted an easier class.
- I only registered for the class in case I didn't get into another course that I intended to "crash."

This term, "crashing" courses, is common on most college campuses (the precise word may be different at your school). Similar to party crashers, the term in college also refers to uninvited guests — in classes. Students who can't get into a course for whatever reason, and decide to attend that class, anyway, are "crashing," or hoping the professor will add them to the course.

There are many reasons to crash a course:

- Many classes are full. The only way to get in is to show up, in case some people drop the course or the professor decides to add extra students.
- Sometimes, students attempt to persuade the professor that they should be admitted into a course, even though they have not satisfied the prerequisite or passed a placement test. Be careful, though. You never want to get in over your head, when the rest of the class is one step ahead from the start.
- Students are unable to register beforehand, so this option is the only way they can get their classes.

Many times, though, it is simply not possible to get into a specific class. *Determine the likelihood of getting into a course early on, because the longer you spend trying to crash the course, the less time you have to try to get into another class.*

For example, what if you try to crash a course for two weeks, and find that there are too many students, and the professor absolutely won't let you in? You run the risk of not finding another suitable course. Or you may get into another course late, so you have to catch up with the course material, readings, and assignments.

Many people at almost every school "crash" courses at sometime or another. However, use your best judgement in deciding when "crashing" can work, or when you should use another option to add a course.

Dropping and adding courses does not always involve "crashing." Many times, you can drop one course, and get into another course with no problem. As early in the semester as possible, like the first few days, decide what courses you think you should drop and which you should add. Usually, dropping and adding works the best when dealing with G.E. classes with many alternative choices. When taking major courses, the requirements are usually more specific and less flexible.

Dropping and adding should not be used as an easy way out of difficult courses. You may be tempted to get out of courses because they seem difficult, because the teacher does not seem interesting, or because you are nervous about some aspect of a course — like public speaking. Keep in mind that you gain a great deal from challenging yourself, facing your fears, or simply sticking it out because you are interested in a course or know that the instructor is great.

Dropping and adding courses is also a good way to avoid staying in classes which make you feel very uncomfortable or may jeopardize your G.P.A., if that is important to you. For instance, if you are in a biology elective that is made up of all science majors, you may want to look for a more suitable biology elective. Or if you are taking a math elective, and everyone else in the course has taken higher levels of preparatory classes, you might want to take a preparatory class before jumping in to that level.

A friend of mine registered for a political science class, and during the first session, the professor asked how many of the students planned on attending law school. The entire class, except my friend and two other people, raised their hands. Needless to say, my friend was out of that course after that session. Note that she was not very interested in political science. She had other choices to satisfy the same G.E. requirement.

If you are at a school where registration for classes is difficult, a good strategy is to sign up for extra classes. Later, drop the classes you don't want. For example, register for six classes, and if you get all six, drop the two you like the least (if you want a 16-unit semester). If you don't get one or two of the classes, you still have enough units for full-time status. This approach will not work at schools where special permission is necessary to register for more than a certain number of units during a semester.

Stay on track towards graduation by taking courses that count towards G.E. or major requirements. Also, try to select courses that you find interesting.

2. Pass/No Pass

At my school, this policy allows students to take three courses with a "pass/no pass" option. This option gives the student credit for the course if they earn a passing grade. However, this grade does not calculate into their G.P.A. Another form of this policy is called "credit/no credit."

Usually, this policy does not apply to courses required for a specific major. To get the "P", or pass grade, a student must earn a C- or better. If a student receives a "NP", or no pass grade, which is lower than a C-, then he or she does not receive credit for the course. However, the "NP" still does not calculate into the student's G.P.A.

In order to take a course "pass/no pass" at my school, students had to initially register for the class "pass/no pass." If they did not, changing this grading option could only be done during the first three weeks of the semester.

Once the "pass/no pass" was registered, the grading option could not be changed back to a letter grade. So students could not abuse the policy by registering for classes "pass/no pass," and then changing back to letter grade options later in the semester, if they felt they would receive good grades.

Again, be careful using this policy. I saw many people register "pass/no pass," because they thought a class would be difficult and might hurt their G.P.A. They end up getting A's. So, *make sure you have a valid reason for taking a course "pass/no pass."*

Also, graduate school admissions officers may not look highly upon courses taken "pass/no pass," because this grade is equivalent to a C-, whether or not the student did better.

I ended up taking two courses "pass/no pass." The first time I registered "pass/no pass" was for a Geography class on weather and climate. I decided to take it "pass/no pass" because I had a difficult schedule that semester. I did not want to worry about my grade in that course. Also, I was very interested in the subject, and wanted to learn without the pressure of getting a letter grade.

This option worked out great because the instructor turned out to be confusing and technical. Most students were worried during the semester, trying to keep up with tests and assignments. Ironically, I ended up earning a B+, which was good for that course. However, I had no regrets about taking Geography "pass/no pass," since I could kick back in there for the entire semester.

I took a Philosophy class "pass/no pass" for the same beneficial reasons I discovered after my Geography class. Also, I wanted to test my theory that it was possible to pass almost any G.E. course by just showing up to class, taking notes, and completing the course requirements based on class material (i.e. papers, and exams). So, in addition to the lack of pressure with a "pass/no pass" course, I also enjoyed carrying out my experiment.

I attended every class, but I never did the readings or attended the discussion section. To this day, I have no idea who graded my work for that class. Anyway, I turned in the assigned papers and took the midterm and final. I did attend one review session for the final to see if I could pick up anything I missed from the discussion sections. The result of my experiment? I earned the equivalent of a "B".

However, this test only applied to this particular course at my university. I doubt that I could achieve the same results in every other G.E. course. In some courses, if you miss something important on the readings or from the discussions, you would not earn even a C-. I do believe, though, by doing exactly what I did in the Philosophy course, any student should be able to earn at least a "C".

The "pass/no pass" option for some G.E. courses may be a good way to avoid the stress of struggling for a letter grade, or avoid the danger of earning a poor grade in an extremely difficult course. You may find other reasons why this policy could either assist you or hold you back in some way. Most schools recommend consulting an academic advisor or professor before taking a course "pass/no pass."

3. Transfer Credit

Many schools allow students to take some of their G.E. and major courses at other schools and transfer the credit to their current school. This procedure applies especially to students who attend one school, and then decide to transfer to another school.

After transferring, previous credits may be accepted by the new school. However, at my school, many students found the transfer credit policies to be very tough. Many previous courses from their other schools were not accepted.

Most schools list specific courses that transfer from other schools. So students who attend either a community college, or other university, with the intention of transferring, can find out which courses will be accepted at the new school.

Students can use transfer credit opportunities to their advantage by taking a G.E. course at home during the summer or at a less expensive school. Since I attended a private university, the savings from enrolling in a G.E. course at a public university or community college were immense.

Another popular strategy is to take G.E. courses at a public school, then transfer to the school of your choice for the final two or three years to receive your degree. This method can be advantageous for many reasons.

- Students save money at a less expensive school for two years.
- Students enjoy a less difficult courseload for two years.
- Students stay close to home for two years before going away.
- Students have the opportunity to perform well, and possibly transfer to a better university, which may not have admitted them out of high school.

If you do attend a school for two years and plan to transfer, there is no guarantee that you will be admitted to the school where you apply. Also, two years at a different school may make the adjustment to a more prominent school quite challenging. You have to spend more time than other students, getting used to the routine, coursework, and lifestyle of your new school. After all, most people have already been there for two years.

The summer after my sophomore year, I took a science G.E. requirement, Astronomy, at a community college. The class cost about $1,800 less than if I took the same class at my school. Additionally, I could take the course in my hometown, and complete the requirement during summer.

Before enrolling in the class, though, I asked the credit evaluations office at my school to verify that the Astronomy course would be accepted at this school for transfer credit toward my G.E. requirements. I received this verification in writing.

I observed these reasons for taking transfer courses.

- The class was less expensive than at another school.
- The student could take the class at home during the summer.
- The class at another school had a better instructor.
- The class was easier at another school.
- The student wanted to try out a class at a specific school to see if he or she wanted to transfer there.

Remember, *if you plan on taking a course at a different school, check with your own school to make sure G.E. or major requirements can be met.*

4. Waivers

Sometimes, students can waive certain required courses or prerequisite courses by taking placement exams.

At my school, placement exams determined where incoming students stood in their foreign language, science, math, and writing skills. Through these tests, students could place out of required courses, bypassing certain prerequisite courses.

For example, to meet the foreign language skill level requirement at my school, students were required to demonstrate proficiency equal to at least three semesters of a specific language. If students met this standard on placement exams, they did not have to take any foreign language courses.

I passed out of the first level Spanish course, but had to take the second and third level Spanish courses. Other students might have placed into the first, second, or third level courses, or out of foreign language requirements altogether, depending on their results on placement exams. So *you might want to brush up on certain subjects before taking placement exams.*

Think of it this way. You can spend a short amount of time preparing for placement exams, and save a whole semester or more worth or work. If you have the opportunity to pass out of skill level courses, or prerequisite courses, give it a try. You can use the extra space in your schedule to take more interesting courses.

5. Incompletes

The "IN", or "incomplete" grade, was given at my school when a student did not complete the necessary amount of coursework to receive a letter grade. For example, if a student missed a large portion of the class, did not turn in a major assignment, or missed an exam, he or she may have received an "incomplete."

The incomplete, unlike the failing grade, can be erased. My school's catalogue states that, in order to remove an incomplete, the instructor must notify the student and department of the remaining work, the procedures for its completion, the present grade in the course, and how much this work factors into the final grade.

Also, *this policy only applied to students who needed to make up unfinished course work because of an emergency or illness.*

A friend of mine arranged with an instructor to complete unfinished coursework during the summer. She had a skiing accident that resulted in missed classes and assignments. The instructor knew my friend had a hard time keeping up. However, not all professors are as sympathetic and understanding. Most professors have a "tough luck" attitude. In other words, they expect students to complete the coursework on time without excuses.

6. Disputing Grades

Grading in most classes is a highly subjective process. For courses such as math, the grading process is obvious. In other courses, though, students may feel that the grades they are given are unfair. And in case you're wondering, not every poor grade is unfair, if it's based on reasonable grading standards.

However, some instructors issue grades based on their prejudice toward a given student. Or some professors have inconsistent and illogical grading procedures. Either way, *students can dispute grades they feel are unfair or malicious.*

At my school, the appeals procedure for grades begins with the instructor. If the student and instructor cannot settle the issue, the matter is referred to a department chair, and even to a director of the academic department in question. This process could involve written appeals and formal hearings.

I did not encounter anyone who went through this part of an appeals process. However, I knew many students who disputed grades directly with their instructors. Most of the time, instructors are willing to discuss and resolve the situation.

"There are three kinds of grade disputes in my classes.

One is essay tests. If students can find where points should be given, I give them those points, if I agree.

The second is multiple choice questions. If students feel there are one or more alternative responses for a certain question, I have them submit a written answer explaining why these answers could be considered correct. If their answers are valid, I give them those points.

The third is course grades. I have never had anybody dispute a course grade in my two years of teaching. If I encountered an unresolvable dispute between the student and myself, I would take it to the head of the department and have them listen to both sides. Then I would honor their decision to resolve the dispute."

> — *Scott Swearingen*
> *Assistant Instructor, Introductory Sociology*
> *University of Texas at Austin*

Throughout my college career, I disputed either final grades or assignment grades four times. Two of the grades were changed. However, I only questioned grades if I felt they were unfair, or if I honestly did not understand how the grades were determined. And if I found the instructor had an objective basis for issuing a specific grade, I immediately accepted it. I never disputed just any low grades. If low grades are fair grades, there is no argument.

Double check that the grades you receive are tabulated correctly. In one of my courses, the instructor simply issued the wrong grade. I called the T.A. who issued the grade. She quickly apologized for the mistake and changed the grade. So don't be afraid to inquire about a grade, if you have a legitimate reason. Most instructors want to be fair. They want to know if their students are confused or unhappy.

In one case, I found out two semesters later that my former T.A. from Philosophy class changed my grade for the better. I guess the T.A. had initially issued an incorrect grade.

This change was encouraging. My T.A. acknowledged a mistake, and handled the inconvenient administrative process of changing the grade. I imagine that she felt that she did the right thing. Ideally, you shouldn't have to worry about challenging the grades you will be given, but always know your options, in case you feel a dispute is necessary.

II BEGINNING

Here's an inside look at the first year of college, beginning with the summer before first classes.

A. New Student Orientation/Registration

Hopefully, you can take advantage of a new-student orientation offered at your school during the summer before you begin classes. This session is separate from the orientation week, which is the week before classes start.

New student orientation provides students an opportunity to become familiar with the campus, meet other incoming freshman, and register for fall classes. Your school will notify you of such programs, or you can call the admissions office and ask.

You may have the opportunity for special personal assistance when choosing your first year courses. At my new-student orientation, we were split into groups. Each group met with academic advisors who helped us individually figure out what classes to start out with.

Unlike most high schools, which basically tell you which classes to take, colleges or universities offer a vast array of courses in many different fields, required courses for different major fields of study, and prerequisites or test requirements for certain courses. This process can be overwhelming, especially at first.

If you don't have, or miss, the new student orientation, academic advisors can help you figure out how to register. Word of warning, the advisors usually get bombarded during orientation week and during the first few weeks of the semester. So try to see them before the mad rush.

During new student orientation, or before classes begin, advisors can provide invaluable advice concerning what courses to take for your major. To find the right advisor for you, look up the school academic advisement office or the academic advisement office for your department (if it's separate from other university or college departments) in the official school catalogue or campus directory. Remember that many students don't choose their majors until their second or third years. So the school academic advisement office can be very helpful to undeclared entering students (students who have not chosen majors). These advisors can assist undeclared students in choosing a schedule of G.E. classes in various fields of study that may apply towards the requirements for most majors.

"Beginning students should stick with freshmen classes, and not take classes beyond the level they are prepared for. It's better to get a good start than a fast start.

We suggest taking general education classes, an interest course, and some kind of course or workshop to improve study skills when students enter school."

> — *Tamara Harrison*
> *Academic Advising Coordinator*
> *Northern Arizona University*

You will probably find at your school that most majors require the same basic categories of G.E. classes. For instance, almost every major at my school required students to take basic composition, foreign language, a few science courses, a literature course, a course in non-western cultures, a course in American public life, and an arts course, to name just a few. You can take all G.E. courses for your first two years of school, while trying to decide on a major, and not fall behind — depending on the major you finally choose.

However, if you do this, you may have to take all major courses during your last two years. And if your major is intensive (like Pre-Med), you might have to start taking required classes all over again because certain specialized fields may require totally independent courses of study separate from common G.E. requirements.

Often you must take a class first semester of your first year that is required for your major and which is a prerequisite to your later classes. So, if you have chosen a major, find out what these introductory classes are and register for them.

New-student orientations also give you brief exposure to university life and what your school is like. You will get a feel for the campus and where things are located. You usually stay in university housing, and probably get to sample campus food and see what you're in for.

B. Orientation

This week can be all fun. If possible, forget you're even about to start school. Just meet people, and try to get comfortable with your new home, or new school, if you're living at home. However, try not to do anything that interferes with your ability to start classes on a positive note.

Orientation week is usually just before classes begin. Various programs are offered to help students prepare, such as:

- campus tours
- academic workshops
- social events (dances, barbecues, dorm meetings)
- seminars, and
- other events to introduce students to the social and academic environment at their school.

For commuting students (students living off-campus or at home with their families), you may have to put more effort into getting to know people and your campus, because you will not be as immersed as students living on or very close by.

Orientation week is also the best time to finish getting everything you need before classes.

Basic things to get:

- folders for note-taking in class
- folders for handouts and class syllabi (outlines of your courses, which are provided by professors or teacher's assistants)
- highlighters
- pens

You may also wish to purchase your books at this point. However, many people decide to wait until at least the first class session before buying books to make sure the titles in the bookstore are the same as the professor's requirements. Always double-check the edition number of your books to make sure they are correct. For instance, a 5th edition is not the same as a 6th edition of the same title. Also, you may find that some books are required and others are optional, in which case you may or may not want to purchase the optional texts.

Another good way to find out what you need at your given school is to ask second, third, or fourth year students. These people have been there awhile and are familiar with the process, but remember that their advice will be subjective. So use your best judgement. If they say something like, "Don't worry about buying books until finals," or "Only show up to class if they count attendance," you may question the validity of their statements. Do they sound like somebody you want to be taking advice from?

During this time, you will probably struggle to feel comfortable and understand everything going on around you. At times, you might be slightly more impressionable than usual. Realize that it takes time to adjust to the new environment and lifestyle. Allow yourself time to settle in. It won't be long before you get used to college life. Regardless, as orientation week comes to a close, you have to face the reality that you actually start your college career soon. This might be the most exhilarating, energizing, and exciting period of your entire college career, so take in as much as you can.

Another good idea is to find all your classrooms sometime during orientation week. Running around completely lost on the first day of classes is not the best way to start, especially if your campus is very large. In the most extreme cases, instructors may drop you from the class, if you do not attend the first session and do not contact them ahead of time. Every school has specific attendance policies for you to consult.

C. Financial Aid

Since I am not an expert on financial aid, *it is in your best interest to consult prospective school financial aid offices and speak with counselors who can explain specifically what you need to do.* However, I will outline some general procedures to be aware of, if you intend on applying for financial aid.

Without scholarships and financial aid, I would not have been able to attend the University of Southern California. So, this benefit may also be your saving grace. *The most important thing to concentrate on before entering school is making sure you complete all application forms, submit them by the prescribed deadlines, and correct any mistakes right away.*

Your first step will possibly come as soon as you fill out your application for admission. Usually, a school will ask you to indicate whether or not you plan on applying for financial aid. If you do, then make sure you check that box on the application.

That school will most likely send you all the necessary forms to apply for financial aid. If not, call the school's financial aid office and request that the forms to be sent as soon as possible.

Do not wait to hear whether you're admitted before you begin the financial aid application process. Sometimes, the deadline for applying passes, before students are notified about admittance. You should go through this process for each school you may attend. Priority is given to students who apply before the deadline. If you apply after the deadline, you will only be eligible for the remaining funds — which may not be much.

Two main applications usually initiate the process. One is for your school's financial aid office. The other, and perhaps more important, is required by the College Scholarship Service.

Financial assistance is determined through the information on the College Scholarship Service form. Many different financial aid packages are provided for students who demonstrate need. These packages may include federal and state grants, scholarships, or loans, and school-sponsored scholarships, loans, grants, or fellowships. Many students are offered college work-study status, which enables them to work part-time to help earn part of their financial aid award.

Other loans and scholarships are available through private lenders or organizations. High school counselors and college financial aid advisors will know where to find information regarding these other options.

Financial assistance in college is another reason why students should take academics seriously. Many scholarships, grants, loans, and fellowships are based on academic results. As my grades improved in school, so did my scholarship awards.

D. Classes

Ready or not, here you go. On the first day of classes, you will probably be both excited and nervous. You'll ask yourself a million questions: "Am I ready for this?" "Should I really be here?" "Do I know where to go?" "Do I have everything I need?" So on and so on. Just relax. Realize everyone feels the same way, and it doesn't last forever — if you feel this way at all.

Also, understand that you're in college now, and things are definitely going to be different. You may not have friends in all your classes, or even know anyone in some of your classes. In many larger classes, attendance is not taken. Often, the professor will never know who you are, or if you ever come to class. You will probably not meet for class everyday in a given course. I believe that the system is designed to treat students more like adults, and less as juveniles incapable of handling responsibility. This responsibility is in the form of freedom to do as you wish, and also be held accountable for your actions, which may be a little overwhelming for some students.

For students living on campus or close to campus and away from home, there are no parents pushing them along and overseeing their progress. No one makes you wake up and go to class. Professors will expect you to keep up with assignments, but they usually do not check to make sure. You have to feed yourself, although most schools have meal plans which provide breakfast, lunch, and dinner on campus.

"You learn a lot about yourself. You learn to be more assertive, to take control of your life, to handle problems yourself, and to approach roommates, resident advisors, or apartment managers with problems. You no longer have your parents to fall back on all the time."

> — *Brooke Grona*
> *Orientation Advisor*
> *University of Texas at Austin*

"It's a burst of freedom. Some students are shocked to find out they need a daily calendar to manage everything."

> — *Leslie Carpenter*
> *Student Orientation Leader*
> *University of Michigan*

"There's the fact that students have never been in an environment with so many people the same age. There are constant distractions — always a basketball game going on, people playing Nintendo, or going out. Self-discipline becomes a big issue."

> — *David Cathcart*
> *Resident Assistant*
> *University of Notre Dame*

In short, you have to take care of yourself in almost every respect. You may not have to worry about working to pay your bills just yet, although you have to make sure that your bills are paid. For many students, college is the effective middle road between parental dependency and the "real world." However, many students must take jobs to support themselves through school, and have to balance both worlds.

With all these "extracurricular" concerns, getting through your classes may seem easy. However, completing your courses is still your main objective. Hopefully, you will pursue this objective with success in mind.

Your basic G.E. college courses will be structured in a similar manner. Specific details, like amount of reading required, number of papers, and level of difficulty, will vary from school to school. However, here is what you can expect in most of your G.E. courses.

1. Days

General education classes at my school usually met for three one-hour periods (actually 50 minutes) a week, with an additional one-hour (or 50 minute) lab or discussion period. Another basic G.E. class meeting schedule is for two 1-1/2 hour periods a week with the same type of lab or discussion. For example, a typical class might meet on Monday, Wednesday, and Friday from 10:00 a.m. to 10:50 a.m., with a lab or discussion that meets on Tuesday from 4:00 p.m. to 4:50 p.m.

At my school, each unit of credit represents 50 minutes of class time per week. Therefore, four-unit classes must meet for a minimum of four 50 minute class periods each week. The combinations for class periods are numerous. However, the above mentioned are the most common.

When you consult your school's class schedule to register, you will find the number of units each class is worth, when and where each class meets, and who teaches each course. (Sometimes, the instructor is not listed in the class schedule.) To get a class schedule, call the admissions office and have them send one. Or pick one up at the admissions office or campus bookstore. Or find a copy in most academic departments on your campus.

Here's an example of the typical information provided in a class schedule. (Usually, all the courses for each department are listed consecutively.)

Course Number	Course Title	Units	Class	Hour/Day	Instructor	Room Number
101	Intro to Basic Astronomy	4	Lec 44345 Dis 44346	11 MWF 9 M	Jones T.A.	SHH MLH
205	Intro to Japanese History	4	Lec 74552	11-12:20 TTh	Nielson	SMH
140	Modern Philosophy	4	Lec 24443	4-6:30 Th	Clark	MLH

— Legend —

Lec	=	Lecture
Dis	=	Discussion section (or lab section). You must register for both the lecture and discussion section for a total of 4 units of credit.
SMH	=	Smith Hall of Humanities
MLH	=	Miller Lecture Hall
T.A.	=	Teacher's Assistant

Class numbers are used for registration purposes and usually do not have anything to do with the type or level of a class. (Not to be confused with the course number, which does indicate the level of the course.)

Also located in the schedule of classes is the schedule for final exams. This section informs you what day and time your final exam will be held at the end of the semester for each class.

When choosing your courses, consult the schedule of final exams, so you can avoid having many exams on the same day, or even more importantly, so you aren't stuck at school until the last day of finals before Winter break or Summer vacation. For students living far away from home, the final exam schedule is also helpful when planning travel arrangements at the end of each semester.

Here's an abbreviated example of a final exam schedule. Actual final schedules usually provide exam dates and times for every class — according to the regular meeting days and times during the semester. Also, your school may list exceptions to their schedule for certain courses.

Schedule of Final Examinations

Classes Meeting	Examination Day	Hour
8:00; 8:30 MWF	Thursday December 17	8:00 - 10:00 a.m.
11:00; 11:30 MWF	Tuesday December 15	11:00 - 1:00 p.m.
9:00 or 9:30; 10:00 - 10:50 TTh	Monday December 14	8:00 - 10:00 a.m.
6:00 or any class after 6:00 p.m. meeting once weekly	December 11 through December 17	7:00 - 9:00 p.m. first scheduled class period

2. Units

Students must complete a certain number of course units to graduate. A specific number of these units are from courses in their major. Each class has a designated number of units. At my school, most G.E. and major courses were 4 units each — 128 units, or 32 classes, were required for a bachelor's degree.

For example, to receive a degree in a certain major, a student might have requirements similar to these:

- Nine courses (36 units) in the specific major. A minimum of five courses must be at 300-level or above.

- Complete G.E. requirements — 13 courses (52 units). These classes will come from a combination of broad educational areas of knowledge specified by your school. (G.E. requirements usually vary with each major and each department.)

- Additional elective courses, or courses for a double major or minor, to equal 128 units.

In the Journalism major (my major), students were required to take 33 units of major courses. The reason for the odd number of 33 was because the Journalism School classes at USC were only 3 units each to make room for courses in another major or minor. (Journalism advisors strongly recommended having another major or minor to complement Journalism.) Each university and each major department has different requirements for units required for graduation.

Under the 15-week "semester" system at my school, the typical course load per-semester was 16 units, or four classes. To be considered full-time, a student had to register for a minimum of 12 units in a semester.

Under 10-week "quarter" systems, the typical semester load is usually 12 units, or three classes. Eight units are commonly required for full-time status. Each school may be slightly different.

Financial Aid Consideration

Full-time status is crucial in receiving student loans and scholarships. Students who register with under 12 units do not usually qualify to receive many student loans and scholarships. Or they are provided with prorated financial aid packages, if they are eligible. And, if students drop below 12 units during the semester, they sometimes have to forfeit loans or scholarships they were scheduled to receive. Check with your school's financial aid office to understand all the requirements for receiving and keeping financial aid disbursements.

3. Numbering System

College courses also have a unique numbering system. The USC Catalogue explains that 000 - 100 numbered courses are preparatory and do not count towards a degree (however, students do receive unit credit). 100 level classes are first undergraduate year courses. 200 level classes are second undergraduate year classes. 300 level classes are third and fourth undergraduate year courses. And 400 level classes are also third and fourth undergraduate year courses. For example, a first year course might be Astronomy 100.

The numbering system at my school was not extremely strict. Many first year students took 200 level classes, and second year students took 300 level classes.

4. Class Structures

When you walk in your first class, you may notice things are run differently than you might be used to. In basic courses, you have a professor who lectures to the class. The class and room size will vary at every school. My first-year classes ranged in size and location, from a giant auditorium with 500 students, to a large lecture hall with 200 students, to a small classroom with 18 students, to another small classroom with 13 students sitting at a rectangular table.

A. Lecture Courses

During a lecture, the professor usually does not take attendance. Students are accountable for showing up and taking notes on their own. The first few sessions are important to ensure your place in the class, and receive the class syllabus, which is essential for the course. The syllabus tells you everything that will happen in the class — course objectives, assignments, and the schedule for mid-terms and finals.

Many lecture courses also have lab or discussion sessions once a week. These sessions are almost always conducted by teacher's assistants (T.A.'s). Labs or discussions allow students to discuss or expand on issues from the lecture material, ask questions, and occasionally complete additional assignments.

Keep in mind that the T.A.'s often grade all the coursework throughout the semester. So you might want to know and understand these people.

The best way to become familiar with T.A.'s is to attend every discussion or lab session and visit them during their office hours. Most universities require T.A.'s to hold weekly office hours.

During this time, they are available to discuss course material and questions. At my school, T.A.'s often spent hours in their offices alone, because no one would show up.

> "Those who come in during office hours are in the minority. I can explain the material in much greater depth. Students can learn a lot more in 10 minutes of conversation than by listening to someone from the back of a lecture hall."
>
> *— Seth Crook*
> *Teacher's Assistant , Philosophy 101*
> *University of Southern California*

These labs/discussions are usually the only place to find individual attention and guidance regarding course material and requirements. Sometimes, T.A.'s consider attendance and participation at these lab/discussions in determining the final course grade. These factors usually account for about 10% of the final grade (the exact percentage should be indicated on the course syllabus).

During the course of the semester, you will get a feel for which lab/discussions not to miss and which sessions you can get away with a few absences. However, you must take full responsibility for any sessions you fail to attend. You might miss a surprise quiz, change of test date, or change of paper topic. If you do miss any class or lab/discussion period, make sure you find out what was covered.

Many students get a phone number of at least one other classmate on the first day of class, in case there's an emergency. For every class, you should try to get at least two or three classmates' phone numbers as soon as possible. When you have questions or problems with assignments, papers, or exams, other students can sometimes provide the best advice and support.

B. Small Classes

An alternative to lecture classes with lab/discussions are lectures in small classes that do not have T.A.'s and are taught by the professor. The professor may take attendance. He or she also grades all the materials. In my first year, I took two basic required courses that were small classes, and run by the professor in a manner similar to high school. The classes were Composition 101, the first year writing course, and Spanish 150, the second level Spanish course. Consult section on First Year Courses for details of my classes and assignments.

C. Small Lectures

Another alternative to the lecture class with lab/discussions, are lecture courses without lab/discussion periods, but with T.A.'s who grade all coursework.

When there are no lab/discussion periods, the best way to ask questions of T.A.'s, or even professors, is during their office hours. Like T.A.'s, each professor is required to hold office hours at least once a week.

"The students just don't come in enough. Any teacher in any subject will be happy to rattle on all day about their subject.

There is a direct relationship to students who come in during office hours and success in my classes. The best students, and the students who have improved the most, have been willing to come in and discuss issues in their papers — both good and bad.

It's one of the best resources students have, and they should use it more."

> — *David Morse*
> *Assistant Lecturer, Freshman Composition*
> *University of Southern California*

At first, you will probably worry about understanding and keeping up with coursework. However, I found that many students' concerns eventually evolve to a point where they worry about such trivial things as waking up for early classes and staying awake during long lectures. The adjustment period will most likely be short, after which you become familiar and comfortable with the structure of classes and routine of coursework.

5. Coursework

Most college students ask similar questions about classes before they register: "How many papers are there?" "How many pages do the papers have to be?" "Do you have to show up to class?" "Is the class easy?"

Through my four years, I noticed many similarities among most of my G.E. classes. The following explanation of coursework is based on G.E. classes open to all majors.

At my school, G.E. courses were divided into nine different categories — The Natural World (Sciences), Non-Western Cultures, Western Culture I (Historical), Western Culture II (Social Trends), American Public Life, Empirical Approaches (Human Beings and Society), Ethical Approaches, Literature, and The Arts. In addition, most students in my class were required to meet skill levels for Composition, Foreign Language, and Mathematics.

For most majors, students were required to take at least one class under each category. Fortunately, we could choose between about 40 course options for each requirement. For example, to complete a course for Non-Western Cultures, a student could take any of a number of specified courses in subjects like Anthropology, Comparative Literature, East Asian Languages and Cultures, Fine Arts, History, Political Science, or Religion.

Science courses do not generally fit the pattern I will discuss, because the coursework varies with each field of scientific study. Most science courses for G.E. are offered separately from those required for students in that major. Science major courses often require an extensive background in science, high proficiency in scientific techniques, and more rigorous coursework in preparation for upper-division (higher level) science courses.

As with most science classes, you can count on reading and memorizing a great deal of information, and possibly applying scientific techniques to exams, assignments, and/or a weekly lab that accompanies the lecture.

To give an example of my first year biology course (and what a syllabus looks like), here's the marked up syllabus from my first semester of college. As with most syllabi, this one provides the weekly assignments, text for the course, and exam dates (we received a separate syllabus for the laboratory section of the course).

As noted in the section on First Year Classes, this biology course was for science majors (pre-med specifically). So don't let this example frighten you. Most students could choose a much easier biology course for non-scientists.

Exam - bring student I.D. - No. 2 pencil - Clip board [ZBo-2A]
A-F (new stags)

LECTURE SCHEDULE & READING ASSIGNMENTS: GENERAL BIOLOGY 106 (Fall, 1988)

Text: <u>Biology</u>, Wessels and Hopson, 1st Edition, 1988, Random House

86

Sept.	5 (M)	Labor Day - HOLIDAY
	7 (W)	Introduction, pp. 2-21 *before Friday*
material includes lab	9 (F)	Reproduction of Eukaryotic Cells: Mitosis, pp. 196-207
	12 (M)	Reproduction of Eukaryotic Cells: Meiosis, pp. 207-217->CRM Movie: Mitosis & Meiosis
	14 (W)	Mendelian Genetics, pp. 218-237->Film - Genetics: Mendel's Law
	16 (F)	Inheritance Patterns & Gene Expression, pp. 237-257
	19 (M)	Inheritance Patterns & Gene Expression (continued);Humans genetics,pp.334-357
	21 (W)	Classification of Organisms, Viruses & Bacteria, pp. 458-483
	23 (F)	Photosynthetic Protists and the Fungi, pp. 485-492, 506-526
	*******LAST DAY TO DROP WITHOUT MARK OF "W"********
	26 (M)	Multicellular Algae and the Bryophyta, pp. 528-542
	28 (W)	Tracheophytes--from Club "Mosses" to Ferns, pp. 542-548;Transport, pp.694-701
	30 (F)	Gymnosperms, pp. 550-557
Oct.	3 (M)	Angiosperms, pp. 557-565; Reproduction in Flowering Plants, pp. 665-680 >23
	5 (W)	Plant structure and function, pp. 642-663, 680-691, 701-710 > 41
	7 (F)	Regulation & Response in Plants, pp. 712-731> 18
	10 (M)	WRITTEN EXAMINATION #1 (7:30 - 8:50 a.m., Bovard Auditorium)>0
	12 (W)	Protozoa and Porifera, pp. 481-603, 568-571 > 14
	14 (F)	Cnidaria, Ctenophora, Animal Symmetry & Germ Layers, pp. 571-577, 597-601>10
	17 (M)	Platyhelminthes, Protostomes vs. Deuterostomes & Blastopores, pp. 577-589>12
	19 (W)	Nematoda, Rotifera & Annelida, pp. 582-584 >2
	21 (F)	Mollusca, pp. 597-601; Arthropoda, pp. 589-593 > 18
	24 (M)	Insects, pp. 594-597; film->Patterns of Survival> 3
	26 (W)	Insects (continued)>0
	28 (F)	Echinodermata, pp. 601-603>2
	31 (M)	Hemichordata, Urochordata & Cephalochordata, pp. 603-612; Pisces, pp. 612-619 (16)
Nov.	2 (W)	Amphibia, Reptila & Aves, pp. 619-631 >12
	4 (F)	Mammalian Origins & Primate Evolution, pp. 631-639, 1216-1241>33
	7 (M)	Natural Selection & Population Genetics, pp. 1010-1030 >20
	9 (W)	Adaptation, Speciation & Population Genetics, pp. 1032-1076 > 44
	11 (F)	Films->Genetics: Patterns of Inheritance; Patterns of Diversity >0
	14 (M)	WRITTEN EXAMINATION #2 (7:30 - 8:50 a.m., Bovard Auditorium)>0
	16 (W)	Behavior: Stimuli, Learning, Orientation & Navigation, pp. 1170-1192 >22
	18 (F)	Behavior: Stimuli, Learning, Orientation & Navigation (continued) >0
	21 (M)	Social Behavior, Sex Roles, Communication & Animal Societies, pp. 1194-1214 (20)
	23 (W)	Ecosystems, Elements & Cycles, pp. 1078-1093 > 15
	*******LAST DAY TO DROP WITH MARK OF "W"********
		THANKSGIVING RECESS: November 24-27
	28 (M)	Energy Flow & Trophic Levels, pp. 1093-1107 > 14
	30 (W)	Growth & Dynamics of Populations, pp. 1129-1148 > 19
Dec.	2 (F)	Interactions Among Populations, pp. 1129-1148 > 0
	5 (M)	Interactions Among Populations (continued), pp. 1150-1160 >10
	7 (W)	Adaptations & Mimicry, pp. 1160-1169 >9
	9 (F)	Ecological Communities, pp. 1109-1127 >18
	12 (M)	Ecological Communities (continued) >0
	14 (W)	Biogeography, pp. 446-455 > 9
		CLASSES END ON DECEMBER 14th

★ — 19 (M) FINAL WRITTEN EXAMINATION (7:30 - 9:30 a.m. - Bovard Auditorium)

52

Another exception to G.E. courses are foreign language and mathematics courses. These college courses at my school are structured much like high school. In math, you go through chapters, complete homework assignments, and take quizzes and tests on the course material. In foreign language classes, you have homework and writing assignments, quizzes and tests on course material. You will practice speaking, either in class or in discussion sessions.

These topics aside, most G.E. courses will come from a variety of other fields. When describing the basic coursework for G.E. courses, I am referring to these other types of classes.

At my school, a typical G.E. course assigned weekly readings of somewhere between 50 and 150 pages, two required papers of between 4-6 pages, a mid-term, and a final. However, the combinations of coursework any given professor may require are innumerable.

From almost any G.E. class, you can expect at least two papers, one mid-term, and a final. Other variations of the above basic requirements could include more shorter paper assignments, one long research paper instead of two or more papers, two or possibly three mid-terms, or some kind of specialized project in a specific subject. For example, in a Cinema-Television/Film course, you may have to direct a scene for a film or make a short film of your own.

Sometimes, these projects are in addition to paper assignments. Sometimes, they take the place of papers and exams. However, projects are the exception in G.E. classes. The coursework in most of these courses will be somewhere near the above description of the basic G.E. course requirements.

E. Major

Declaring a major is an important, and often difficult, decision that every college student faces.

From the time you enter college until you declare a major, you will probably spend a great deal of time thinking about what your major should be. I strongly suggest that you consult other people during your decision making process, such as career counselors, academic advisors, professors, teacher's assistants, family, professionals in your field of interest, and friends.

"The most important aspect in deciding on a major is whether it is something you're interested in.

Then you should consider what it takes to graduate with that degree, and what opportunities will be available when you graduate."

> — *Tamara Harrison*
> *Academic Advising Coordinator*
> *Northern Arizona University*

"College is a chance to explore new areas. It's a time to experiment with many different areas of interest.

It's great if you're 100% convinced about pursuing a specific career. It's also great to have an open mind, instead of deciding on the most practical major and overlooking something you really enjoy."

> — *Rob Agee*
> *Former Guest Relations Staff Member*
> *University of Southern California*

Here are other factors to consider when thinking about a major.

- Will attending graduate school be necessary in this field?
- Will further preparatory courses be required before beginning major classes?
- Do you feel you have the skills and motivation to succeed, or at least get by, in this field?

"We encourage students to take a broad range of courses at the very beginning to explore. A change of major is very easy. Most unhappy students are those who decide before they're ready — and when they take a course in their field, find it hard or uninteresting."

— *Hannah Gilman*
Senior Academic Advisor
University of Massachusetts at Boston

Many students do not make their final decisions on a major until they have taken courses in a variety of subjects during their first two years.

III GETTING STARTED

1. Here You Go

For years, you can't wait until the day you finally move on to college. Whether entering straight out of high school, or after a short hiatus, the thrill is the same. However, the stakes are much different. Almost everyone has to attend high school. Yet not everyone chooses, or is able, to attend college. So, if you're going, you must feel proud and eager as you prepare to prove yourself among the education system's elite.

At first, everything is new and possibly shocking. Whether you're living at home or going away to college, you'll soon find that things aren't the way they were in high school (Thank God!). Some things about college may seem wonderful, and some things may seem overwhelming or unpleasant. However, this will most likely be your life for the next four to five years, so get used to it.

2. There I Went

The Summer Before

As I began trying to figure out what I would need to bring to college, it finally sunk in that this was it — I was going away to school. Okay, so it was only 100 miles to the north and a two-hour drive away, but it still wasn't home. Thankfully, my school scheduled a new student orientation during the summer. So, many freshman, including myself, had already become slightly familiar with the campus.

The night before I left, of course, I didn't sleep at all. In fact, I felt sick to death. It took me about two days to even eat normally. Before leaving, I double-checked a list sent by my school that detailed everything students needed to bring: Sheets, blanket, phone, extension cords, desk lamp, alarm clock, and daily necessities (clothes, toiletries, medication, etc.). Students living at home get to bypass this whole ordeal. But don't let going away frustrate you. Part of the fun of going to college is being there. Living on campus is also a very important element of the learning experience of college.

3. Arriving

After checking into the dorms and putting everything away, my parents left. It was Y-O-Y-O (you're on your own) from this point on. From here on out, I would make all the decisions about what things I would do, how I would do them, when I would do them, and who I would do them with. Although, in my case, I had this independence all through high school.

As it worked out, my roommate, whom I had never met or talked to before, showed up just before I did. So we sat there, with both of our parents helping us get things organized, saying our "Hi, how'ya doin'?," and "Nice to meet you's."

> "We encourage new roommates to sit down with each other, and even with both their parents, and just shoot the breeze. They usually find they have something in common.
>
> Most kids had their own room at home. Now they have to put up with the little things, like a roommate having a class an hour earlier and getting up and making a little noise.
>
> They should go in knowing there are going to be things that come up, and not expect things to be just like home. We encourage people, if they have a problem, to say something and not bottle it up. Finally, they should listen to their roommates when they bring things up."
>
> — *David Cathcart*
> *Resident Assistant*
> *University of Notre Dame*

If you're lucky, you can find out about your roommate ahead of time. If so, you can get in touch with him or her, and break the ice before living with that person for a whole year. Also, you can discuss who'll bring what: posters, stereo, T.V., phone, answering machine, computer, typewriter, microwave, or if it's an apartment — dishes, utensils, furniture, and cookware.

My roommate and I realized early on that we didn't really hate each other, but we also didn't necessarily like each other a great deal. So, as with many other roommate pairs, the only times we saw each other were in our room.

On the first day of check-ins during orientation week, everybody was a little nervous, but I could tell most students were desperately trying to hide that fact. Everyone reacted slightly different. Some kind of hid in their rooms and ate alone at the dining halls. Others started drinking and hitting the Greek Row (street where most fraternity and sorority houses are located) the very first night. I would say the majority of people during the first week were eager to make friends and feel comfortable in a new and exciting environment.

Certain questions popped up innumerable times:

"Where are you from?"

"Where are you living?"

"What's your major?"

"What classes are you taking?"

During orientation week and the beginning of school, I seemed to ask these questions a million times. I answered the same questions just as often. It was pretty fun, though. I met more people from different places with different interests than ever before. With this process of meeting people comes the great possibility that most people will hit it off with some or several of the people they come across.

As with any change of environment in life, most people have various reactions during the first few weeks of school.

"Students are often worried about the competitiveness. I'd estimate that 70% of the students in my orientation groups say they didn't work that hard in high school. They might have to push themselves in college.

There's a shift at many schools from being at the top of their class in high school to being one of the many. It makes it easier to know that their peers are in the same situation."

— *Leslie Carpenter*
Student Orientation Leader
University of Michigan

"Many people are shocked by the differences among the student population. They find that not everyone else has the same background. College is a wonderful chance to meet new people they wouldn't have had the chance to meet at home."

— *Brooke Grona*
Orientation Advisor
University of Texas at Austin

Orientation week was probably the most fun I had all four years. My fears died down as I met a lot of people I liked. I realized that this greater independence was awesome. We were everywhere, doing whatever we wanted. My advice is to just relax, make sure you have everything ready for first classes, and enjoy yourself before school starts.

.

IV First Year Classes

As classes began, I realized that the system was not so confusing. In every class, I received a syllabus that explained the class and what we would do for the rest of the semester (my school was on a 15-week semester system). So from the first day, I knew what my assignments would be for the rest of the semester and when they were due. Sometimes, instructors changed syllabus information slightly during the semester. However, this change usually didn't cause major problems.

Now came the hard part. It was totally up to me to make sure I got everything done. The days of teachers overseeing students' progress and making sure assignments were completed were all over. How much, and how well, I studied was under my own control. At first, I didn't know how to study in college. I had to test the ground myself. I wished I had known more about what was ahead.

I started by attending every class session and taking furious notes, as if everything the professor said would appear on a test. Classes were not all that bad. Fifty minutes was just about right to avoid absolute boredom. When the lectures were interesting, the 50 minutes would fly by.

I met many of my friends in classes. It's always great to have somebody in each class you can talk to — especially if you're confused, miss a class, or want a study partner.

A. Fall Semester

Here is my first semester schedule:

(Note: M—Monday, Tu—Tuesday, W—Wednesday, Th — Thursday, F—Friday.)

• If there is just one number for the class time (i.e. 10), this means that the class met for the regular 50 minutes (i.e. 10 - 10:50 a.m.). Also, I will use "dis" as a substitute for lab to indicate discussion sessions.

> Biology 106 — Principles of Biology I
> MWF 8
> Lab W 1-4:30
> 4 Units

(Refer to section on "Coursework" for actual copy of my course syllabus.)

Pre-med biology — I thought I would start off pre-med because it sounded so prestigious. However, I realized studying sciences makes my head pulse.

Requirements for this course included about 80 pages a week of reading, 10 quizzes, two mid-terms, and one final.

Quizzes were given in the weekly lab session run by a T.A., in which we also used scientific methods for physical observations and experiments.

Tests were multiple choice, and required memorizing tons of facts, ranging from the various levels of life on the planet to animal behaviors. Most exam questions came from lecture material, but some very specific questions were from the reading assignments.

This course counted toward one of my science G.E. requirements. However, easier biology classes for non-science majors were available.

Although I read and highlighted all the assignments, I always missed test questions from the readings because I failed to go back over the information or make study notes.

I ended up doing all right in the class. I met a junior who helped me memorize course material about two weeks before exam time. This person did very well in the class. She outlined chapters from the reading, prepared study notes from the lecture material, and studied previous exams which the professor made available. Some instructors expect students not only to be familiar with class material, but with test formats also.

Cinema-Television 190 —
Introduction to the Study of Cinema/ Television
T   2-6
Dis Th 9
4 Units

Cinema 190 covered a G.E. requirement for the arts. This class was a very popular elective among freshman and sophomores. Why? Two out of the four hours of lecture were spent watching movies, such as "Singing in the Rain," "East of Eden," and "Die Hard."

A discussion period, run by a T.A. who graded all the coursework, was scheduled once a week to analyze elements of filmmaking. Among the requirements were a 4-6 page paper and a 7-8 page paper, a mid-term, and a final. I rarely did the assigned readings. However, a friend and I had to go back and look up terms and topics in the book after receiving the review sheets before the mid-term and final. These review sheets outlined the terms, topics, and names to know before the exam.

This Cinema-Television course turned out to be great fun. We viewed and critiqued a different movie every week as we learned various elements of filmmaking. Also, the professor was vibrant and energetic.

Exams for this course were fairly simple. After my friend and I prepared study notes, I simply pored over them for about three days before the test. I utilized and improved on making study sheets for exams throughout my college career. The technique I developed worked very well in all my classes.

Here's my preparation routine for almost every exam I took.

• Start with the first day of class and copy down all relevant information related to the topics on that day.

- Go through the reading for the same lecture period. Add any relevant information not covered in lecture.
- Do the same for every lecture and reading assignment that will be covered on the exam.
- Study the information on the study sheets thoroughly.
- Discuss the topics with friends in the class.
- Relax before taking the exam. To get your mind off the exam, go to lunch with a friend, exercise, watch a mindless T.V. show, or even take a nap. I suggest allowing at least two hours of relaxation before any exam.

This process may seem like a lot of work, but it really isn't that bad. To do well on exams, you have to prepare well. After preparing study sheets, studying wasn't that difficult, because I retained a great deal of information, just from recopying class and reading material. Also, if I made the study sheets a week before the exam, I usually had about three full days to study without pressure, rather than cram.

I admit that preparing study sheets this way is time-consuming, but if you sit down and get it over with in two or three days, you will find it worthwhile and rewarding.

I did very well on both tests, because I was ready for any question.

During the actual exam administration, I used three techniques to help my performance.

- Relax when taking the exam to free the information in my head.
- Write down every relevant idea or fact on each topic. Or include every relevant point when arguing a position.
- Apply what I know to various types of questions.

This last lesson was important. I learned that not every question would be "Define these terms," or "What happened on July 4, 1776?" The exams would often be based on course material, but many essay questions required expanding on various issues or topics.

For example, in a film class, the student might have to apply theories from the course to a film seen outside class. This example is very simple, but the idea is that you have to use what you know of the course material in any situation — that's what instructors want to see.

I did poorly on the first paper, which dealt with filmmaking techniques used in a film seen outside class. Instead of just dismissing the paper, though, I reviewed the comments. I realized the T.A. wanted more direct examples from this particular film to be included in the paper. Some of her comments asked how I arrived at certain points, and where in the film and on what scenes did I base my points.

My plan worked. The T.A. loved the second paper, which had better examples from the films I wrote about. Also, I made sure the paper stayed focused and supported my proposed arguments.

I learned two valuable lessons early on:

- Read the graded comments and determine what instructors are looking for.
- Read my papers over to make sure they are concise and clear.

In high school, I tried to make papers sound good. In college, I found instructors were more concerned about the quality of content than my expression. So I always attempted to make my papers coherent and supported by unique observations.

Spanish 150
MTWTh 12
4 Units

Spanish was one of the skill level courses that students in most majors were required to take at USC. Students also had to meet basic skill levels in Mathematics and Composition. If I did extremely well on the placement exams, I could have passed out of these requirements. But I didn't. This Spanish class was at the second level. So, I only had to complete the third level for the skill level requirement.

Remember foreign language classes in high school? Basically the same thing here. Weekly homework assignments, weekly quizzes, speaking in class, and a mid-term and final exam.

The tests were a combination of multiple choice questions (usually on vocabulary), sentence completions, an essay, and a speaking exam administered by another instructor (not our own instructor, who was already familiar with our speaking abilities).

All I had to do was show up every day, complete the short homework assignments, and study a little for tests. The workload was really minor, if students kept up. As always, many students occasionally skipped class and assignments. These same students usually paid the price when the time came to study and take the tests.

Since the class was not that difficult, some students thought they could get by without any effort. They learned that some easy "A" classes can fly right by, because they underestimate the effect of missing class meetings and assignments.

Composition 101
MWF 10
4 Units

This writing course was for freshmen students, except those who passed out of the requirement, or placed into the second semester Composition 102 class. As stated previously, this class was a required skill level for most first-year students.

I took Composition very seriously, because I knew writing would be a key element to my later success in college. This class involved writing one 3-4 page paper every two weeks, in addition to a mid-term writing assignment and a final essay exam. The intensive writing for this course and the second semester Composition 102 course paid huge dividends throughout the rest of college.

We were given a selection of topics that usually required developing a strong argument to support the claims we introduced in our papers. Besides covering grammar, sentence structure, word use, and overall paper structure, the instructor encouraged students to come up with sophisticated ideas in papers.

I admit I usually don't think that way, but I learned how to do it on command.

Here is the introduction of one of my very first papers in "Comp."

The assignment? Walk around our campus and observe as many things as we could. Then write a short paper based on these observations. Most students just described the physical environment. They described the buildings looked like, how the campus was structured, or anything else that happened in front of them.

Merrick Marino
Composition 101

The University of Southern California was founded in 1880 by members of the Methodist Church. The campus of U.S.C. is abundant with traditional Spanish architectural designs and ravishing fountains. To many, this is the epitome of the perfect college campus and environment. Upon further investigation, though, one may find that within the structure and individuals lies a dissension between power and confusion. The facade of invulnerability faces counteraction with the always prevalent human element of uncertainty.

The large, and carefully arranged U.S.C. campus can seem very intimidating. The reputation of tradition and strength, alone, signify the domineering influence this school has on society. When entering the campus, the visitor's eyes are drawn to the towering buildings that bound in all directions. The Phillips Hall of education stands tall; Bovard Auditorium is stern and foreboding; Doheny Library is reminiscent of the glamour in <u>The Graduate</u>; Von KleinSmid Center with the entire world in it's grasp; and the Hancock Foundation Building with it's extension to the entire city. Within view lies the Shrine Auditorium, which houses the captivating Academy Awards and American Music Awards; the Los Angeles Coliseum, the center of worldly attention in 1984 as the site for the Summer Olympic Games; and the interest provoking Aerospace Museum. With this kind of prosperous environment, it is no wonder that publications like the London Times Sunday magazine will release an article entitled "the University of Spoilt Children."

Instructors want to see thoughtful papers. Show them that you have carefully considered the issues you address in any given paper. Demonstrate your ability to communicate your ideas in an organized and persuasive manner.

In many of my classes instructors stated that they did not care as much about what students argued in their papers, as long as they argued well. For example, an instructor who supports the "Pro-Life" stance could still be impressed by a strong paper that argued for "Pro-Choice." Be careful not to diverge from what the paper topic asks.

My writing style improved as the class went on. I expressed my ideas more effectively, and made original observations that made my work stand out.

Unfortunately, I also learned a tough lesson in this course. Going into the final, I had an A-. My instructor had been impressed with most of my work. I figured I had the course wired and could cruise through the final.

I dismissed preparing for this exam. After the final, in the course of two hours, my grade dropped to a B. In short, I received a C on the final exam in part because of my overconfidence, and because I was really not prepared. The exam counted for 50% of the final grade. So I obviously made a major mistake, yet this is how lessons are learned. I rarely took any test or assignment for granted again after this experience.

B. Spring Semester

In my second semester, I was more comfortable with the style of college courses and my grades improved.

> Composition 102
> 3-4:15 TTh
> 4-units

This course was basically the same as the first semester Composition course, except we had longer paper assignments and one long research paper in addition to the mid-term and final.

> Spanish 220
> 11 MTWTh
> 4-units

This third level Spanish course was the last one required to complete the skill level for a foreign language. Again, this course was basically the same as my first semester Spanish course.

> Math 117 —
> Introduction to Mathematics for Business and Economics
> 12 MWF
> Dis T 4
> 4-units

I took this class to fulfill my math skill level requirement. The instructor completed problems on a chalkboard during lectures, based on textbook assignments. During the discussion, we reviewed our assignments and asked questions. We also took ten quizzes during the discussion section.

After the first test, I realized that the math problems on the exams were structured exactly the same as those that the instructor covered in class — only using different numbers. So before tests,

I would repeatedly go over his example problems from class. By noticing his pattern, I could slide through this course, which was great, because I don't like math. Not every instructor has noticeable patterns with test questions. However, always be on the lookout, if they do.

Anthropology 201 — Introduction to Social Anthropology
9:30-11 TTh
Dis 9 F
4-units

This G.E. class was very typical. We had four paper assignments of 3-4 pages each, two mid-terms, and a final. On average, we were assigned about 80 pages of reading per week.

The exams combined multiple choice, short answer, and essay questions based on lecture material and readings. Questions from the readings dealt with issues that came up in lecture. So students could get by doing little or none of the reading assignments.

Our paper topics asked us to apply theories or methods we learned in lecture to our own experiences. For example, one paper assignment was to discuss the theory of rituals and apply it to some ritual in our lives.

Here is the introduction of the last paper I did for Anthropology. I compared various cultures of music in the United States to social cultures around the world. My purpose in this paper was to show how someone could apply the same data gathering techniques of social anthropology to another field.

Through one semester of class, Professor Costin has shown that sociocultural anthropology can be applied to many things in one's life. Culture can often be overlooked or not appreciated as it is always prevalent in social activities. From the information presented in Professor Costin's course, I am now able to associate the anthropological method of data gathering to my own field of interest. Involved in the music industry are many of the same aspects of culture as studied in Anthropology. In taking the anthropological approach to study the complexities of making music, I am rewarded by a deeper understanding of the lifestyle I hope to lead.

In sociocultural anthropology, the main form of data collection is through field research. This information gathering involves active participation in the culture to be examined. The gains of immersing oneself musically to many varying forms and techniques of music are immense. Looking at each different type of music as a different culture, the best musician is the one who is capable of adapting to each different style. There are many who concentrate on one form of music, such as reggae, yet those who will be in highest demand are those who are proficient in many different areas. Similarly, in anthropology there are many who study and become experts in the knowledge of one culture, yet it would seem that the best anthropologist must also have knowledge of many different cultures. Seeing that not all cultures are the same, studying single groups only will not provide a degree of comparison with which one could gain a wider scope of understanding cultures in general.

Music Performance 201 — Drum Set
11 T
2-units

This class was my favorite during the first year. I played drums most of my life before college, and was slightly depressed at the possibility of losing playing time while in school. So I registered for a 2-unit course for drum set instruction. Not only did I get credit for the course, but I also studied jazz drumming with a Grammy Award winning drummer and used the school's drum set whenever I wanted.

I took the drum class for four more semesters. This class also allowed me to get away from studies occasionally. The individual lessons were extremely rewarding. If you have space in your schedule, enroll in an elective that you enjoy and that takes you away from the pressures of school for awhile.

V TIPS FROM EXPERIENCE

As an entering student, the adjustment to college life and studies took some time.

Here are some noteworthy lessons or tricks of my college career (beginning with my second year first semester).

1. Take Your Assignments Seriously

During my second year, I got burned on a paper in a philosophy class that I put little effort into. I again made the mistake of becoming overconfident in my writing. I overlooked the only paper assignment for this fairly easy class. Instead preparing my argument, I rushed the paper out and thought I could easily fake my way through. Wrong! The T.A. trashed my argument. It's really frustrating to let what would have been a good grade get by because you were lazy.

2. Extra Credit Opportunities

A surprising event occurred in my Geography 205 class, which also took place during the first semester of my second year.

The professor encouraged the class to attend a guest lecture. He announced that students who attended might get a treat if they did. Many students called the bluff, and didn't show. I decided to go. The guest speaker was incredibly boring and confusing. However, at the end, our professor took down the names of all the students from his class. He then said that we would receive credit for an "A" on our last paper assignment without turning anything in. Of course, the other students who did not go were unhappy with that decision.

This event reassured me that any opportunity to get extra credit was worthwhile — especially if it required absolutely no effort on my part.

Often, professors or T.A.'s allow students to turn in an extra paper, or some additional assignment, to improve their grades. Usually, this practice is directed towards students who are in danger of receiving poor grades.

3. Maybe I Don't Have To Do Everything?

Again during the same semester, I took a Mythology class where I realized from the start that the discussion session and readings were unnecessary. I'm sure anyone who loved Mythology read all they could, but many students bypassed the reading assignments. The reason — the teacher discussed the mythology stories in lecture, and let us know from the first session that everything on the tests would be covered during class. When I heard this statement, I knew I had to just show up to lectures and memorize my notes. Then I would be required to correctly answer the short answer questions on the exams.

Don't get me wrong — I had to study a good deal, but I knew exactly what to study. So every minute I spent studying helped improve my score.

This process is what I mean when I refer to maximizing your time and minimizing your effort. It's difficult, because you have to make constant judgements on what is important to study for exams. It's the same process for papers — learning what to include and what the instructor wants. But you have to take these necessary steps in all your classes to be prepared.

- Attend class
- Take comprehensive notes.
- Make effective study sheets.
- Budget plenty of time for exam studying. Start at least one week prior to the test.
- Pay careful attention to paper topics and instructor's comments on papers.
- Relax enough to let all you know come out in your papers and exams under timed conditions.

And how do you relax? As discussed earlier, you relax by taking part in activities that release tension and calm your nerves (exercise, music, T.V., resting, hanging out with friends, etc.). Also, you relax when you complete all these steps of preparation.

4. Notice Patterns

Similar to my math course, noticing test patterns helped me turn my performance around in a Journalism course on the history of news in America.

This class met twice a week for two hours. The professor talked endlessly about how major events in American history affected Journalism.

For our three exams, we were given the essay questions one week ahead of time. We could choose two of three essays to address.

The exams also included identification (I.D.) questions on people, places, and events. We were a given a choice of I.D. questions to answer — ten out of fifteen.

This type of test question selection occurred often. Many of my G.E. exams included a choice of I.D., short answer, or essay questions to answer — like 3 of 5 or 7 of 10. I found that if I prepared enough, I would always be able to answer at least the minimum number of questions.

For the first exam, I studied my notes thoroughly for any I.D. questions, and then planned how to write an effective essay on the given topics.

When I learned I did poorly on that first test, I wondered where I went wrong. I looked at other students' tests, and figured out that scores were determined solely on the number of facts included in the essays and identification questions. There were no comments on writing style or quality, because those aspects didn't matter as much in this course. Instead, there were only check marks above every fact included in the essays and I.D. questions. The total number of checks added up to give the total score for each exam.

So after receiving the essay questions for the second exam, I memorized as many facts as possible to include in my answers. I studied all my notes for the I.D. questions. I narrowed down the time in studying for I.D.'s by figuring out the type of I.D.'s included on the first exam, which were significant names and events from lecture material. Then I concentrated on similar items for the second exam.

There was a lot of material to cover, which took many hours of studying, including making comprehensive study notes. Again, my time was used to study exactly the material I needed in order to score high on the test. As a result, I did extremely well on the second and third exams.

Here are some I.D. answers straight from my original exam booklet. Notice the check marks above the facts.

This exam was written in a "blue book," or a small blue paper booklet of about eight pages, which many instructors require for essay exams. "Blue books" are just about the right size to fill up in a two-hour exam situation.

5. Know Your Strengths and Weaknesses

I learned to evaluate my academic abilities, and adjust my study time accordingly in certain courses. This strategy helped me get through a Classics course on Ancient Drama during my sophomore year.

This class met twice a week for 1-1/2 hours. We were assigned many Greek and Roman tragedies to read. The exams were very tough, due to the amount of reading.

In addition to short answer questions from the lecture material, we were given passages from our readings from which we had to identify the play, the author, the speaker, where the passage occurs, and the significance of the passage.

Unfortunately, I was unfamiliar with this style of exam and did not do well at first. As usual, I prepared from the lecture material. However, I just relied on my memory for the reading material. I figured that I could recall enough from the readings, because we discussed the plays in class. Besides, I read all the assignments. I quickly learned that I am not one of those people who remembers everything they read. Not even close.

For the next exam, I reviewed the readings and made notes on the major characters and major events. Also, I recalled what was discussed in class about the plays. I ended up doing better in the course after the first test.

More importantly, I realized that some types of exams are not as easy for me and require more effort. I believe most students have strengths in certain areas, such as reading comprehension, writing, memorization, or problem-solving. Sometimes, these students can put less effort than others into certain types of exams or assignments. It's a fact of life. *The best thing to do is figure out your strengths and weaknesses. When they arise, adjust accordingly to spend more or less time and effort.*

Or avoid those classes which may be difficult or less interesting for you. However, people often sacrifice grades for knowingly difficult courses. Usually, this trade-off occurs when they are really interested in the subject, or absolutely have to take such a course for a G.E. or major requirement.

VI FIRST YEAR LIFE

During my four years in college, I found that many experiences were shared by the majority of students. These observations are based mostly on students living at or very close to school and not at home. They were just beginning their college careers.

Most college students are moving away from home for the first time, which can be overwhelming. At first, almost everybody loves the fact that they can do as they please when it comes to going out, studying, or cleaning their dorm or apartment. As can be expected, many problems arise when students take advantage of these freedoms, and lose focus of their studies and responsibilities.

My first year, I lived with other freshmen. The students that ran into trouble had difficulty turning down offers from friends to do other things when they should have been studying.

Like high school, there is a great deal of peer pressure in college. Friends and classmates constantly try to convince each other to miss classes or delay assignments. This part of the college experience is what I call "life education."

> "Peer Pressure takes on some very positive roles, and can also take on negative roles. If an individual has formalized their sense of self-identity, they will have an easier time dealing with peer pressure."
>
> — *Dr. Thomas DeStefano*
> *Director University Counseling and Testing*
> *Northern Arizona University*

When we started, my classmates and I attempted to balance both our "life education" and formal education. In other words, we struggled to keep up with our coursework and adjust to our surroundings. At the same time, we tried to maintain control of our personal lives and activities.

> "Adjusting to the social environment is probably as important to most students as adjusting to the academic environment. There is a gradual sense of adjustment and adaptation each does on their own. This is a very positive experience for most students."
>
> — *Dr. Hugh Pates*
> *Psychologist*
> *University of California, San Diego*

"Students should acknowledge that this is a transition, and with that comes uncertainty. They should be easy on themselves.

Students often come to school with certain expectations how to be in the new environment. If these expectations are high, students might be depressed or frustrated if they don't meet them. They should identify whether they're being negative in their expectations."

> — *Gary Tedeschi*
> *Staff Psychologist*
> *University of San Diego*

A reminder from my section on recommendations — in order to succeed, do your work during the time you plan to do your work. When you finish putting in the necessary effort, then indulge in your favorite extracurricular activities. This trade-off is essential to succeed in almost any work situation — school or career. However, I saw many freshmen who did not prioritize their studies complain when they received low grades. It is hard to concentrate on studies when there are so many opportunities for more fun things to do — especially when students are on their own, without their parents to monitor their every move.

Here is a typical scenario that is similar to many situations I observed during the first year of school.

One Boring Fall Semester Night

7 p.m. on Tuesday night. Joe has a paper due tomorrow at 4 p.m. He's worried because he hasn't started to write, and knows he's already behind schedule. Midterms just ended last week, and he wasn't able to prepare for them effectively, because he

and his girlfriend (now ex-girlfriend) Stacy, were fighting constantly about whether or not Joe should go away next summer. So, Joe knows his grades are in jeopardy.

At this point, Joe is on the verge of throwing in the towel for the whole semester. The pressure from school and from Stacy are overwhelming. But he's determined to get through it, and raise his grades.

Now he's ready to write his paper. Joe has read the paper topic, and has the direction for the paper in his head. It's 7:15 p.m. when Joe finally sits down to write. Fortunately, his roommate, Steve, decided to go out, and won't return until later. Joe's fingers first strike the computer keys at exactly 7:24 p.m. He's on a roll with two sentences down, when in walk Pete, Lisa, and Ann. Joe is especially vulnerable to invitations to go out, because of his loneliness after Stacy — and in this case, his possible interest in Ann.

Pete says, "Hey Joe, we're hitting Stonie's, wanna go?"

Stonie's is a college bar just across the street from campus. Joe knows a lot of people are there, ready to celebrate, since most midterms were over last week.

"No way, man. I have this paper due tomorrow at four."

Lisa approaches the computer, and squints to read the screen.

"What's the paper on?"

"Philosophy. We have to discuss whether we really exist or whether there's an evil deceiver who is tricking us into believing we exist."

Lisa laughs. "Easy. Just say we don't exist, and therefore, neither does your paper or school."

"Yeah, right."

Joe avoids eye contact with anyone, trying to resist the temptation to go out. He knows that if he goes out, he will have to miss both of his classes tomorrow to finish the paper. And he probably won't have enough time to write a very good one.

Ann walks over to Joe and puts her hand on his shoulder. Joe smells her perfume, and can't help but look up at her. He's in trouble now.

"Come on, Joe, we'll just stay awhile. If you're not having fun, you can just come back to your room."

Joe is at the crucial deciding point. He either heeds his better judgement and finishes his work. Or he follows his immediate desire to get away from his schoolwork and have some fun. Now begins the ten-minute battle between responsibility and carelessness.

During Joe's mental jockeying, he puts off making a commitment. The game begins. They pressure. He attempts to resist, although he welcomes the conflict.

"I can't. I'll have to miss my classes tomorrow to finish the paper. And I don't think I did well on those midterms last week."

"Don't worry about it. You can make it up in finals."

"I don't know."

"Yeah, besides I have two papers due Thursday that I haven't even started. Don't be such a stresser."

Joe is slowly giving in. "What's better?" he asks himself, "sitting here all night writing this paper or having some fun, while I'm still young enough to enjoy it?"

The pressure continues.

"You're not gonna write, anyway. You're gonna end up calling Stacy, and talking all night."

"Shut up. No, I won't."

Joe knows this statement is probably true. His defenses are broken down. They've won.

"What the hell, I probably wouldn't get anything done, anyway."

"Alright!"

"Let's hit it."

Joe saves his two sentences on the computer, and gets up. They walk out, laughing and ready for the night's festivities.

* * *

Believe me, similar situations occur all the time. Most college students face difficult decisions that cause conflict between social, personal, and academic priorities. These dilemmas emerge from high school to college, and on to later years.

The above story is based on some situations I observed and experienced during my four years of school. Students are not always ready for the amount of control they have over their lives and futures.

College is not only a matter of getting an education, but also of learning to strike a balance in your life. Learning to set and achieve personal and school-related goals can be the most rewarding result of the college experience.

The possible results of decisions students make in similar situations to Joe's story are endless. For instance, like Joe, students may sacrifice their studies for other opportunities.

Sometimes, students don't even need other people to pressure them. They just don't do their work. During college, and the years that follow, students are responsible for the decisions they make. So college is a good time to begin using your full capacity to make decisions you feel are in your best interest.

The backgrounds and reasons for each student's behavior in their social and academic lives are innumerable. Regardless, when my class began our college careers, we were all expected to react and adjust quickly and effectively to a new lifestyle.

Students with difficulties in any areas of college life should consider seeking assistance.

From personal to academic problems, counselors, advisors, tutors, and student organizations are available at most colleges and universities. Plus, friends and family can also sometimes offer help or support.

Depending on the size of the school, any entering student is almost guaranteed to see other students experience many similar ordeals.

A. Observations

Here are some observations of first year students from myself, and a few other knowledgeable sources:

- Students who missed their hometowns and friends.

"Many students feel as if they lose the social network they had in high school and at home, and the closeness of their family."

— *Larry Perez*
Resident Director
University of San Diego

- Students who loved getting away from their parents and hometown. For some people, a change of location is just what the doctor ordered.

- Students who missed their sweethearts and called them long-distance almost every night. One guy I knew called his girlfriend in Oklahoma (we were in California) every night. He ended up transferring back home after the first month of school. Unfortunately, I also witnessed many long-distance relationships break up during the first year.

- Students who became involved in their first serious relationship. The whole area of relationships and break-ups caused more personal problems for people than anything else I observed in any of my four years.

- Students who could not resist the opportunity to party any night they wanted. This condition is common at many colleges, since students gain the independence to pursue such lifestyles. However, many new students find that such lifestyle choices result in academic probation rather quickly.

- Students who couldn't keep anything clean — especially their clothes and their rooms or apartments. I can't count the number of people who wore pink clothes for the first few months! (Hint — separate whites from colors when washing clothes). One guy in my dorm slept on the floor, because he used his bed to pile his heaps of dirty clothes.

- Students who hated their roommates after about one week of living with him or her. Here are some problems that roommates encounter and possible solutions.

  "One who comes in late, while the other likes to go to bed early; one who has a lot of company, while the other likes to spend time alone; one who gets into the other person's side without permission; one who plays their stereo or T.V. too loud; one who doesn't care about sharing, but the other has a hard time with it.

  Addressing problems right off the bat is so important. It's also the way you say it. If you say something spitefully, they might get offended, and keep doing things just to get back. Make sure you're in check, and are doing whatever you can to make the situation work out. Try to be open-minded. If you do all this, your roommate won't have a reason to get upset at you."

  — *Veronica Satterfield*
  Resident Advisor
  Syracuse University

- Students who enjoyed the college environment and experienced as much of it as they could. Whether they loved their classes, their majors, their classmates, their school's social activities, or the fact that they were working towards better futures, many students can't help but get involved in college. Some people just can't get away from school. They often end up coming back to receive additional undergraduate degrees, or graduate degrees. Or some of these students just put off finishing their undergraduate degrees for as long as possible, so they can stay in school. Fifth and sixth-year-seniors were not unheard of on my campus.

- Students who stressed out about everything, especially getting good grades. Some students would actually go into depression, if they received any poor marks in any of their classes. Many first-year students were really afraid of not excelling in college. Unfortunately, many students base much of their self-esteem on their grades.

Here's an example of someone I saw constantly stressing out.

Stresser

Every time Phil watches the television show "Seinfeld," he feels like a younger version of the character "George." In other words, he worries about anything and everything.

Last week, Phil and Teresa studied together for their political science midterm. Today, they got their tests back during lecture. Phil earned a "B." Teresa earned an "A-."

When Phil saw Teresa's score, he immediately sunk into a state of gloom for the rest of the lecture.

"Phil, what's wrong?" Teresa asked.

"Nothing," Phil snapped back.

"Well, you sure look ticked off. Listen, if you're freaking out about your grade, don't worry. A "B" is great. Besides, if you want an "A," you still have a great chance with two papers and the final left."

"Yeah, whatever." Phil maintained his intense and angry stare straight at the lecturer.

"Okay, Phil, whatever," Teresa conceded.

When the lecture ended, Phil bolted from his seat without a word to Teresa.

Teresa decided to stop by Phil's apartment later to talk.

Hearing the knock at the door, Phil knew it was Teresa, but he didn't want to deal with anyone at the moment. So he kept looking blankly at the T.V., hoping Teresa would leave. He felt like his whole college career was collapsing.

Teresa yelled from outside, "Come on, Phil, at least let me in."

Phil glanced at the door for a second before lazily getting up. When he opened the door, Phil noticed that Teresa looked concerned.

"Hi Phil, I just came over to make sure you're okay."

"Yeah, I'm okay. I'm just mad as hell. Oh, come on in."

Teresa walked in, and sat at the dining room table. Phil slumped on the couch in front of her.

"Phil, I honestly don't understand what's the big deal."

"Well, I studied twice as much as you did for the test, and you still did better."

"What? We studied together the whole time." Teresa was obviously shocked and slightly upset.

"Not really. After you left each night, I studied for an extra two hours. I just wanted to make sure I didn't screw up one of my first tests."

Teresa laughed at the anxiety Phil created for himself.

"Yeah, I know how you feel, but you're a little over the edge. I think you'd do a lot better if you just relaxed."

"That's just the way I am. Seems like I'm always on edge." Phil sat up and slowly clutched his face with his hands in frustration. "I can't handle failing in school. I feel like such an idiot right now. I mean, I barely ever got B's in high school."

Phil remembered that the orientation advisors said that competition in college would be tough, since most new students were high achievers in school. Now the grading curves in classes, from A's to F's, would be redistributed among people who were used to getting A's and B's all the time. Still, he never thought he would suffer.

"You're right," Teresa said. "You're putting way too much pressure on yourself. Have you ever heard of overstudying?"

"No." Phil looked at her in desperation.

"Well, you need to settle down and not worry so much. That's probably why I did better than you on this test. I was prepared, but I also didn't study more than necessary. I didn't even look at my books the night before the test. What did you do?"

"I studied until two in the morning."

"I'm telling you, Phil, you've got to change your attitude before you have a coronary."

"I know, you're probably right."

"We're all in the same boat, Phil. It's gonna be tough, but we'll get through it all."

"Yeah, I just wished we were there already." Phil smiled at Teresa who returned the gesture.

"Except when we finish, we'll probably wish we were back in school."

Phil laughed, and shook his head to acknowledge the irony.

"Life can be just a little too confusing."

* * *

Here's another story based on my experiences with people who faced identity problems in college. At the time most people enter college, they are still trying to discover themselves. In the midst of various pressures and influences, the search is often tough.

Many people take advantage of the college experience to develop as stronger individuals. Or some people see the new environment as an opportunity to test new identities. Unfortunately, students sometimes find themselves unhappy with who they are and who they associate with.

Like any other time of life, students can turn things around, and take control to make their lives positive and fulfilling.

Change

They made the arrangement at their high school graduation — they would visit each other during the first semester of college. It was tough saying good-bye that summer, but Holly and Deborah were both excited about going away. So Holly arrived to stay with Deborah in her dorm, traveling 200 miles from her own campus for the weekend.

Back in high school, Holly was on the tennis team, but didn't participate in much else. Deborah, on the other hand, was a cheerleader and active in student government every year. Despite their different interests, they remained good friends.

Holly knocked on the door of room #409 in Hillman Hall. When the door opened, Deborah jumped at Holly, and gave her a big hug.

"Hey, buddy!"

Deborah released her embrace, and led Holly back into the room. Deborah and her roommate had contacted each other over the summer, and coordinated color schemes for their room. So the bed linens, towels, cups, and window shades were a matched combination of green and pink. Surprisingly, the room was spotless when Holly entered.

"This is nice. Your dorms are nicer than ours."

Holly dropped her suitcase on the floor, and lounged on Deborah's bed.

"So whatta' we have planned? Any parties tonight?"

Deborah sat next to Holly on the bed.

"I don't know. I haven't gone to very many parties so far."

Holly stared at Deborah, surprised.

"What? You never missed a party in high school."

"I know, I guess I kinda burned out. I've actually been going to a lot of music clubs."

Holly grinned at Deborah, realizing something about her was not quite the same as three months ago.

"Like what?"

"Well, let's see. I went to see a Latin percussion band two nights ago, and last week I saw this incredible modern jazz group."

Deborah stood up from the bed, pulling Holly up with her. "What?" Holly asked with a quizzical glance.

"I've got to show you the campus."

Deborah took Holly down the center thoroughfare. On each side of the walkway are large buildings with students and faculty coming in and out of the entrances. Although there were numerous bike riders speeding by in both directions, both Deborah and Holly were undisturbed. They were now used to this form of campus traffic.

"So what else have you been up to?" Holly asked, as they walked by the Humanities building.

"Not much, I've been studying like crazy. What about you?"

"Oh, well, I've been doing a lot with this guy, Mike, that my sorority sister set me up with."

This time, Deborah displayed the look of surprise.

"You joined a sorority?"

"Surprised?"

"Kind of. In high school, you never really got into groups or anything."

Deborah stopped, and sat on a bench, just as they approached the intramural track and field. About fifteen students walked or jogged around the track, while a pick-up soccer game took up the field.

Holly joined her, and they watched the activities on the field.

"Wow, I guess we've both changed a little since we left."

Deborah flashed her a friendly smile.

"Happy so far?" Deborah looked at Holly, awaiting a response.

Holly peered at the sky, pretending to ponder the question. Although, the answer was obvious.

"Totally! I've met so many people I like and get along with. It's just such a nice change from the same old people at Clearview High."

Deborah laughed in agreement, then put her arm around Holly. With a mockingly serious expression, Deborah faced Holly.

"We've come a long way, little girl. Now back to Mike . . ."

Deborah and Holly strolled arm-in-arm toward the school bookstore and dining hall.

". . . does he have a cute roommate?"

Holly giggled, and playfully shoved Deborah.

"Some things haven't changed a bit!"

* * *

Don't be surprised if you see many of the things discussed in this section happening around you. Or even if you find yourself experiencing some of these things. College is probably one of the greatest opportunities in your life to learn and enjoy yourself.

I often heard people tell me to take full advantage of my college years, because they would probably be some of the best years of my entire life. I can't help but believe they were right.

B. The Greek System

With many activities, clubs, and organizations on campuses, the only limitations concerning which to choose are usually time-related. Various campus groups range in size and purpose.

- Common interest groups, like the American Advertising Federation, Undergraduate Students Psychology Association, and American Institute of Architecture Students

- Cultural/Ethnic organizations, like the Black Student Union, Asian-Pacific Student Alliance, Latino Business Students Association, and Armenian Student Association

- Sports clubs and intramural teams, like lacrosse, softball, and volleyball

- Student publications, like campus newspapers and yearbooks

- Student councils, committees, and government

- Community service groups

Student affairs offices inform students about organizations on campus, and how to get involved.

An organization that is totally unique to colleges and universities is the Greek System. Since the Greek System has such a strong historical background on many campuses, there are certain terms, procedures, and regulations that separate it from other elements of campus life. So this section on the Greek System introduces new college students to an original part of student life.

However, this section is just informational, and does not advocate nor discourage involvement in the Greek System. Also, some schools may not have Greek organizations at all (in particular — two-year community colleges and vocational/trade colleges).

Here is a general overview of what to expect at your school. The best sources for information regarding fraternities, sororities, or other Greek organizations is through your prospective school's office for Greek life or student affairs office.

As you enter your first year of college, you will probably hear about fraternities and sororities. Many schools send information on how to get involved with Greek organizations.

When I started school, my familiarity with the Greek System was what I had seen in movies (i.e. "Animal House"). I found a diverse and unique culture of Greek organizations at my college campus. In addition to traditional fraternities and sororities usually associated with the Greek system, check out Greek organizations that cater to certain ethnic and academic aspects of the student population.

Since the decision whether to join a Greek organization is a highly individual process, I won't make a recommendation regarding "going Greek" either way. All I can say is that I didn't join a fraternity, but I enjoyed an active social life and developed lasting friendships. I also have many friends who did join a fraternity or sorority and found their experiences to be equally rewarding.

The Greek system at a given school refers to a number of fraternities or sororities that can be "chapters" of bigger national organizations, or local chapters established at a particular school. These chapters are identified by two or three letters from the Greek alphabet, like Sigma Phi Epsilon, Sigma Nu, Alpha Phi, or Pi Beta Phi. Each chapter may be located in a large house located somewhere near campus, or hold their meetings and events at locations on campus. Either way, fraternities and sororities are referred to as "houses."

A common question students ask each other is, "Are you in a house?" They are usually asking if you are in a fraternity or sorority. At my school, the street where the houses are located is called "The Row." The number of members in each given house varies, depending on the enrollment of a school and the size of the organization.

Active members of each house are simply called "actives." During a formal one or two-week event called "rush," a joint decision-making process occurs, when prospective members decide which houses they are interested in, and "actives" decide who they will invite to join their "house."

During "rush," interested students meet the members of the different fraternities and sororities. Sometimes, "rushees" visit every "house," before deciding which fraternity or sorority to "pledge."

When I was at school, sorority rush was held during orientation week before classes began, while fraternity rush was held two weeks into the semester.

If "actives" of the sorority or fraternity decide to invite a "rushee" to join their organization, they offer a "bid." Most bids are extended at the end of the one or two-week long event. The rushee accepts or declines the bid.

If they accept, they will either begin their pledge semester, or become a member right away. Most houses across the country require at least one semester of involvement, or "pledging," after the bid is accepted, before full membership status is granted.

While "pledging," many fraternities and sororities require their "pledges" to perform various tasks as part of their initiation into the house. These requirements may include working for the house's national or local philanthropy, meeting with the actives, required weekly study hours, learning the sorority or fraternity's history, learning the Greek alphabet, and various forms of house maintenance (washing dishes, cleaning, and decorating for parties). The old-time stories of horrible acts of mental or physical abuse to pledges, called "hazing," is now illegal at all schools. However, some "houses" are known to secretly continue some of these traditions.

During my new-student orientation, some orientation group leaders gave great advice on Greek organizations. They told us to wait until at least a semester, or even a year, before making the move to join a fraternity or sorority. Then you have time to adjust to your new academic and social environment. Also, you can attend some events, and talk to pledges and actives to see if you're really interested in pursuing Greek life.

The responsibilities of a pledge semester, in addition to the already difficult elements of a social and academic transition, are sometimes too much to manage right away. The most common problem students face when joining a Greek organization is spending more time with their house than on schoolwork.

Another consideration of joining a fraternity or sorority is money. Joining these organizations is costly, and often the monthly dues are quite high. So this factor may present a financial hurdle for some students.

During my four years of school, and in discussions for this book, I compiled a short list of some advantages and disadvantages of joining a fraternity or sorority. Keep in mind that the merits of either lifestyle is often a source of heated debate between Greeks and non-Greeks at many schools.

Greek Advantages:

- Meet many people, make friends, and establish a support group right away in a new environment.
- Maintain an active social calendar of meetings, parties, and activities with fellow fraternity/sorority members.
- Choose to live in a house, instead of a dorm or apartment.
- Be involved with numerous community service opportunities.

Greek Disadvantages:

- Be responsible for a large time commitment, especially during pledge semester.
- Experience social isolation from other students when only associating with "Greeks."
- Pay expensive monthly dues.

Independent Advantages:

- Keep a flexible social calendar and self-determined time commitments.
- Maintain greater independence by meeting more diverse students.
- Avoid having to learn that silly Greek alphabet.

Independent Disadvantages:

- Experience difficulty in meeting people and developing support.
- Miss out on the networking that fraternities and sororities usually provide during and after college.

Take advantage of the great opportunities to experience new and exciting things at college. So do yourself a favor, and look into the possibilities.

VII ATTITUDE AND ATMOSPHERE

I survived and succeeded in college by telling myself constantly that it didn't matter how I did, just as long as I finished. My attitude towards school was that all I could do was my best, and accept the results of those efforts.

So for every paper I wrote and test I took, I put very little pressure put myself for results. There was relatively no pressure from my family, either. Besides, coming out of high school, I was not a great student. So everyone, including myself, really hoped that I would just graduate from college!

I realized early on that my education was very important to me, but my personal wellness was equally important. So I refused to make life miserable in order to get through in school.

This idea raises a very important topic — balance. Some people can study or work constantly, and never burn out. However, other people, like myself, need a balance between studies and other activities.

These other activities could be any of a number of things, including exercise, hanging out with friends, dancing, skiing, church, volleyball, going to movies, watching television, going away for weekends, or reading. These activities took my mind off school and studies for awhile to give me some breathing room, so I didn't feel totally consumed by my academic commitments. Then, *when it came time to concentrate on my studies, I worked much more efficiently.*

My attitude in school also comes from my easygoing personality. I simply believe it does no good to take anything in this world too seriously. We are here for such a short time. Why spend the time worrying? I put more thought and effort into my development as a person with good character. I always felt that all the top grades in the world, or the best job in the world mean absolutely nothing, unless I am happy with myself as a person.

So my success in college resulted from my techniques for studying and my attitude toward school. My success definitely did not come from pressure from either myself or my family. If you're going to succeed in college, do it for the right reason — for yourself.

In terms of family, my mother, father, and stepmother were behind me every step of the way. During the first two years they received three typical phone calls every semester.

1) I called home during the beginning of each semester, telling my parents that I didn't think I could pass any of my classes. In Philosophy, Journalism, or Cinema, students raised their hands and sounded really intelligent. I always convinced myself that I was no match for them, and I could not even compete.

Whenever this happened, my parents told me to hang in there. I would say, "Okay, but don't be surprised if I fail out this semester." My worries never materialized.

2) When midterms or finals and papers piled up, I called home to say, "This will be my worst semester ever. I hope you won't be too disappointed." Their reply was always, "Just do your best, and don't go too crazy." My grades were never of great concern to my parents. They were extremely excited when I succeeded, but they would have been equally supportive and understanding, if I was not able to do as well.

In raising their children, my parents provided total freedom to allow each child to decide and pursue their life's interests. Nothing was forced in my household. If one child was interested in education or religion or astronomy, they were free to explore this interest.

For me, education was necessary for the goals I wanted to accomplish. My parents understood my feelings, and offered as much support as they could.

By the way, I have a sister in college, and another brother and sister who did not continue their education past high school. My parents accepted all of our decisions. So this lack of performance pressure from my parents allowed me to approach my education in a manner that was best for myself.

3) Another phone call my parents constantly received was the "I can't decide on a major!" lament. I was not one of those people who knew exactly what they wanted to do from early childhood. In fact, I changed my mind about every two weeks, trying to figure out a suitable major until late into my sophomore year.

As far as I can remember, I looked into pre-med, music recording, jazz studies, human geography, urban and regional planning, cinema- television, and finally ended up majoring in broadcast journalism. My parents encouraged me to look into all the fields I found interesting. They only wanted to know whether it was really what I wanted to study. At the time, their response was frustrating, because I wanted somebody to just say, "Yes, that's it." However, it worked out great, because I eventually made the best decision for myself.

Support from family or friends, or even from yourself, is very important in all aspects of life, but especially during school. It is not as important where the support comes from, as long as some kind of support is there. And if no one provides the backing you need, look within yourself for affirmation and encouragement.

Success was not just in terms of grades, but also what I learned about myself, what I discovered about many academic subjects and other people.

Another attitude that helped me get through school was my "just get it done" attitude towards assignments and studying. *My approach was to always first concentrate on getting things done, then worry about the quality of my work.*

Whenever I did schoolwork, I told myself to finish a paper or study just enough so I could pass a test. This made it much easier for me to get over one of the biggest hurdles in coursework — getting started.

So when I began my schoolwork, I never felt like I had to write a great paper or had to really score high on a test. Instead, I concentrated on completing the minimum, either finishing the paper or studying enough to pass, to get me through the class.

Then, when I finished the minimum amount of work, I could go back and correct my papers, or study more effectively for exams. I found that I always had time to go back, and put more work into my studies, and my first efforts were much better than I thought.

So when I would review, I found that my papers were already organized and only needed revising. I realized that I had prepared better than I thought for exams and only needed reviewing.

However, keep in mind that I also overbudgeted the necessary time for studying, anyway. So what I considered the minimum amount of studying was often what other students considered the maximum time to study. Often, I would go back and hate my papers, or realize I wasn't prepared to excel on an exam. However, I always had time to correct these situations, and still avoid working under last-minute conditions.

The results of this process were, according to my instructors, superior assignments, papers, and exam performances.

At this point, it's time for a confession — I was almost never satisfied with the work I did in school. I thought my papers and exams were terrible. My friends were tired of me saying, "This paper was my worst ever, and there was no way I could get above a 'C'." I honestly thought my work was not at the college level. However, these feelings didn't distress me too much, as long as I put my best effort into the course requirements.

Ironically, I was most often pleasantly surprised when my assignments or exams were returned. These feelings of inadequacy did subside after about two years of good performances in my courses. It was exhilarating to enter my university, doubting whether I would graduate, and end up graduating with top honors. Whether it's expected or not, I will be the first to say that earning high grades and honors in school can be very gratifying.

So the elements contributing to my success involved much more than just my study techniques. My success also resulted from my attitude, and the support of my friends and family. With them, I created a positive atmosphere for studying and for personal growth.

However, I feel that individuals need to create such an atmosphere for themselves in order to succeed in school and life.

For people who just want to do well in school, I suggest consulting Recommendations for Success. And for those people who want to do well in school *and* remain satisfied and happy in the process, I suggest combining effective study techniques with a positive atmosphere for maximum learning and growth.

Conclusion

When I entered college, I had no expectations of high achievement, or any strong desire to finish at the top of my class. However, I learned academic success influences other areas of my life.

Academic achievement usually tells people something about you right away. More importantly, success in college usually does not say anything negative about a person. This success usually indicates that a person has outstanding character traits such as discipline, responsibility, intelligence, motivation, and perseverance.

So many people automatically think positively towards academically successful people, until such a person proves otherwise. On the other hand, people who have not done as well in school usually have to spend extra effort and time, trying to prove that they possess the same character traits.

The objective for most students in college is to get a good education and enjoy themselves. Doing extremely well, in terms of class performance, may not be one of their top priorities. It wasn't my top priority, but I was also able to do it and witness the benefits firsthand.

I secured an internship in the entertainment industry at Paramount Pictures. This department never before had an intern. Paramount's Domestic Television Programming division also allowed me to create my own job duties and schedule. Without my proven academic success, they would probably have never allowed me to begin and develop a new internship position.

I feel that the opportunities will continue as a result of my academic success. I am very proud of my accomplishments. My unexpected college success improved my confidence a great deal.

Academic success is not necessary for people to feel good about themselves. However, I'm sure it helps. I was fairly unsettled before entering college. I can honestly say that I have since taken my life in a more positive direction. Grades alone didn't do this for me. The whole experience did — going away from home, meeting new people, beginning new friendships, proving to myself I could succeed, taking things into my own hands, overcoming many fears about living on my own and competing in the high pressure environment, and developing into my own person.

Right now, I look at an unbelievably exciting future. My academic success has given me many more options. Believe me, there is nothing better in life than having options — especially great options. The more options, the more likely you will find a direction that suits you best.

A last word about academic success — people are just impressed by people who have done extremely well in school. Whether they are students, instructors, family, friends, or employers, people think highly about success at the college or university level.

Whenever my parents tell people about how well I did, they always say things like, "Wow, he should be really proud!" or "That's really impressive."

I personally don't place that much importance on my academic results. (I feel that being the best person I can be in my own eyes is the encompassing goal. Academic success plays a supporting role.) However, it's nice to hear praise. If you play a good tennis game, do a good job at the office, or excel at anything else, it is gratifying to hear other people acknowledge your accomplishments.

A person should do what they feel is best for them. I have expressed many incredible benefits that result from the college experience. However, these views are mine. I suggest that each person pursue what they feel is their most beneficial experience.

To make the best of your college years, start right away. Your first year establishes how the rest of your college career will be. Once you find your key to success in college, the rest is easy — just keep it up each year.

The college environment and academic success in college opened many doors for me, and brought me to a much brighter place in my life. I wish that everyone else can find and enjoy such positive experiences in life in whatever they choose to pursue. When the heart and mind work together, the results are absolutely incredible. ***Find your balance and take off!***

A Note from the Author

We want this book to be the most current, honest, and helpful introduction to college available to incoming students every year. You have the special opportunity to participate in this process. By letting us know how it has affected your transition to college, which sections are the most helpful, and which sections need improvement you can become eligible for prizes, publication credits and more.

Check the boxes of interest to you and mail this page to us for more information.

❏ STUDENT ADVISORY BOARD — Conduct interviews, document current trends in college, attend an all expense paid trip to San Diego for a weekend editorial meeting, and earn publication credit in the next edition of the book.

❏ WRITE-IN CONTEST — Earn prizes and get your submission published. Your input helps us stay in touch with current college trends and needs.

❏ EXTRA COPIES OF THIS BOOK — $12.95 plus $1.50 for handling and shipping. Quantity discounts available.

Please mail to: **College Undercover**
c/o Wharton Publishing
3790 Via de la Valle, Suite 204
Del Mar, CA 92014
(619) 759-1296

I am interested in the **College Undercover** :

❏ Advisory Board   ❏ Write-In Contest

Name:_____

Address: _____

_____

Telephone Number: ( )_____

Name of College: _____

❏ Extra copies ____ copies x $14.45 $_____ My check is enclosed.